The Identity of Purity

A TEENAGE GIRL'SGUIDE TO SEXUAL PURITY

RHIANNA SANFORD

ISBN 978-0-9896895-0-2

Printed in the United States of America

For more information please address:

Rhianna L. Sanford
312 E. Mulberry St.
Olathe, KS 66061

To my husband, for being my biggest fan. To my parents for every ounce of Godly wisdom you've sown into my life. To Nikole for asking me to write a few devotions. Who knew? Lastly, to my former youth pastors and leaders for doing and saying what most won't.

4

Table of Contents

Taya & Taryn,

Yoy girls are worth so so more than you think! Don't ever let anyone tell you any different!

Rhonda

8

Introduction

SEXUAL PURITY: THE FINAL FRONTIER

"FAR, FAR away in a land…" Ok, not really. But sometimes the subject of sexual purity seems like it can only be experienced in a world in another galaxy somewhere! Depending on the environments you find yourself in, you may not even recognize that term. Or furthermore, what "purity" even means.

Purity is actually quite simple to understand if you know the idea or origin of purity. Purity was actually God's design from the very beginning of time – from Adam and Eve to the 10 Commandments, and from the story of Ruth all the way to the days that Jesus walked on this very Earth! God has longed for His children, young and old, to remember purity throughout life. I will admit that, while it's simplistic in its nature and origin, it's not exactly regarded as – easy to grasp. You see, plenty of other messages don't really regard purity…at all.

Many of us females, young and old, somewhere along the way have bought into the story that sexual purity is impossible. "No one expects a girl to stay pure until marriage!" "All the guys want a sexy girl." "He must love me if he wants to sleep with me." Lies like these have influenced many women from youth and have affected how they view and feel about themselves even into adulthood. Often this drives girls to think they're not pretty enough or that they have to do certain things to get attention from boys. Therefore, they begin belittling who God has called them to be and settling for what "seems" like acceptable behavior. Some of this behavior may include, but is not limited to, dressing provocatively, flirting with boys to gain fulfillment of being accepted, and being so emotionally needy that boundaries and standards in general vanish from their lives to get what they feel they're missing.

The real problem with not understanding purity is that it tends to lead to a domino effect of decisions of choosing lesser or inferior options throughout every area of life. When God designed you, He designed you to be fulfilled by being close to Him. He designed you to operate at your greatest ability through following His great and fabulous plan for you. The only way to completely and totally be full of joy and fulfilled throughout your life is tied to how well you understand your Creator and His love for you.

That is why much of this book will not just be about abstaining from sex until you are married to that special guy. It will include that message, but some crucial things have to be approached before one can even begin to understand the **why** behind sexual purity.

Before you can truly be successful at achieving purity throughout your adolescent years (and really, throughout life), you need to be able to correctly answer these two questions:

- What is God's design of purity?
- Why should I care about purity?

By the end of this book, you should be able to answer both questions and be a part of the revolution of young girls choosing to take on God's standard of life over anyone else's.

Sexual purity IS achievable. It IS absolutely possible and shouldn't be thought of as some unreachable concept. Are you ready to experience above and beyond what unfortunately many young girls never get to? Are you ready to draw a line in the rest of eternity and begin the most amazing journey you were meant to live? If your answer is "YES," I'd like to congratulate you! You're on your way to a mind-blowing transformation!

Chapter 1

Purity Briefly Explained: A Thing of the Heart

> *Flee also youthful lusts: but pursue righteousness, faith, charity, peace, with them that call on the Lord out of a pure heart.*
> 2 Timothy 2:22
> (King James Version)

Have you ever watched anyone decorate a wedding cake? I'm amazed at how much detail goes into the designing and decorating of wedding cakes these days! It's tough for me to just write "Happy Birthday" on a cake in icing while people pay hundreds, sometimes thousands, of dollars for the cake-decorating extraordinaire to do incredible things with icing and fondant. They are just so gorgeous! Wouldn't it be nice for the baker if all he had to do was to decorate a cake well?

When a bride is choosing a wedding cake, not only does she examine the perfect design and décor, but she also *tastes* it. If she's going to pay hundreds and hundreds of dollars for a wedding cake, she wants to be sure it also TASTES good to share with all her friends and family celebrating the occasion. If it doesn't taste good, the cake is really a waste and has defeated its purpose altogether.

A cake's first purpose is to be EATEN. That's the heart of the purpose of making a cake, to eat it. The outer decoration has nothing to do with how good the actual cake tastes. But if the baker is mindful to create a tasty cake using good ingredients, the cake will fulfill its primary purpose and intent of its creation. The outer beauty is just an added bonus, but not necessarily important to fulfill the heart of its purpose. I for one know how disappointing it is to bite into a gorgeous cake and find it lacking in flavor and consistency. Most likely I won't eat it all and want to throw it away.

The problem I see in today's young girls is that they're concentrating so hard on making sure their outer selves are accepted that they neglect the most important part of themselves...their heart. They base their importance on the outside rather than the deeper element of what truly makes her valuable. Just as it takes good quality ingredients to make a delicious cake to be enjoyed by all, a young lady should concentrate on acquiring good qualities that allow her to be and do all that her creator created her to be and do. You can be sure that she'll be described as attractive and beautiful as well! But it may not be because of the clothes she wears or how much makeup she wears. It'll be because she possesses so many beautiful qualities that make her gorgeous from the inside...out.

Understanding purity in general is the key for young ladies truly walking in the purpose of who they're supposed to be and what God always intended them to experience. And it begins in the heart. Being pure in heart means to operate in ways that reflect God-like character. Some of those qualities are mentioned in 2 Timothy 2:22. *"Righteousness, faith, charity, and peace"* are all qualities that ooze out of those who look to God to mold their lives, even from young ages. While being young comes with temptations and, as the verse says, *"lustful desires,"* purity can still be achieved.

A concept I must bring to your attention is that sexual purity is actually a PRODUCT of being PURE IN HEART. You can't have sexual purity without a pure heart. Purity is a parent of sexual purity.

When a girl has a pure heart, she will wait to have sex until marriage because she thoroughly UNDERSTANDS WHY she should wait. That knowledge and understanding compel her to live her life in a way where sexual purity isn't even an issue for her. Her heart is laced with quality God-like ingredients that make her one WHOPPING catch, and she acts like it.

> *Achieving sexual purity is one thing, but first you must understand how to apply God's design of purity in **every** area of your life.*

We'll get into this more in the coming chapters. But know this. Achieving sexual purity is one thing, but first you must understand how to apply God's design of purity in **every** area of your life. It's just like before you can decorate a wedding cake, you have to successfully mix up a lick-the-bowl batter of fresh ingredients and bake it to the desired consistency. It doesn't matter how it's decorated when you have achieved the main purpose for the cake. A young lady has to realize what her main purpose and identity are, and that is wrapped within her quest for purity. It can't be found by searching for a boyfriend, husband, the popular crowd of kids at school, or anywhere else. It can only be found as she lives her life according to God's original design. Otherwise she risks being treated like a bad piece of cake and is wasted, thrown out, or treated like trash. And NO girl should be treated like trash.

The transformational keys to purity you read in this book will undoubtedly lead to sexual purity and a WHOLE lot more. So let's make a yummy cake, shall we?

Chapter 2

Recognizing True Love

> *Your love, O Lord, reaches to the heavens, your faithfulness to the skies.*
> Psalms 36:5

Jesus came to the world and pretty much just caught everyone off guard. He didn't look like what everyone thought He'd look like. He didn't sound like what everyone thought He'd sound like. He had to speak in a way to help people understand Him by using stories and parables as parents use nursery rhymes to teach children to understand a moral thought. I think that people expected Jesus to come on a cloud with gold and silver in a crown upon His head. Yet for centuries it was foretold by the prophet

Isaiah that He would come in the form of a babe through a virgin (Isaiah 7:14). God had warned His people about the coming of the **Messiah** (the one who'd come and be their Savior) through prophecies that have been recorded in scripture. Nonetheless, many thought He was nothing special when He came. Can you imagine waiting your whole life for the one thing that was promised to you, then realizing after it'd come and gone that you'd missed

it? Seems sad, doesn't it? Sad but true. It happens all the time. Jesus and His death on the cross many years ago provided a way for us to experience something so great it's hard to fathom at times. Since Adam and Eve sinned in the garden, the increasing amount of sin in the world continued to separate God's people from Him. God was so desperate to redeem His people back to Himself that He sent His son Jesus in exchange for the price of their sin. And it's out of God's unfailing love for us that we still have access to that same salvation today! The Bible actually tells us in 1 John 4:8 that God is love. This means that God is the original maker of what true love is and its expressions through His actions. You could call him the "Architect of Love." Do you know what that

means? It means that you already have examples of
what *real love* looks like!

Have you thought to look to God to see what love
truly looks like? We don't always have the greatest
examples in this world to go by. But the Bible is full
of truth and wisdom to help you learn things that will
keep you from missing out on all the good stuff God
planned for you. When Jesus appeared He stuck out
like a sore thumb! Many didn't like Him, and only
few received and followed Him. Of course, now
millions around the globe believe in Jesus and have
received Him as their Savior. But sometimes God has
something so different in store for you, and it's
possible that you could be clueless about it. You are
the only one who can make the decision as to
whether you'll let it (true love) slip past you or not.

May I recommend you keep the Word of God very
close to you and plant it in your heart? Why?
Because when false thoughts, ideas or messages
crowd you (through the media, schoolmates or
wherever), the Word of God has the cool ability to
cut through them with its powerful truth.

Why is it important to know so much about God?
Well, if you were going to build a house from the

ground up, wouldn't you want that foundation to be strong and safe for you and your family to live in? A correct understanding of who God is will give you a strong and efficient foundation for your life because God is your creator! He is the one who breathed life into you and designed you to be just the way you are! God is omniscient, meaning that He truly knows everything about you. In Jeremiah 1:5, God told Jeremiah the prophet, *"Before I formed you in the womb, I knew you."* And it's the same with you! In the very first book of the Bible, Genesis 1:27 says, *"So God created man in his own image in the image of God he created him; male and female he created them."* It's very important to know who your creator is to be able to live this life to the full abundance and capacity that God,

> *If it doesn't add up with what GOD SAYS about you, take it with a grain of salt. It's just not true.*

your creator, intended. When you know and understand what God has for you in this life, all of the other things that people say – what you see on T.V. or in magazines or hear on the radio – should really just go in one ear and out the other. If it doesn't add up with what GOD SAYS about you, take it with a grain of salt. It's just not true.

Ever play cards? I learned to play a game called "spades" in college. In the game there is a trump card, which is more valuable over any other kind of card. Any card with a spade on it is going to be higher than a card with a heart, club or diamond. The king of hearts could be trumped by a two of spades. Even though the number two in a normal case would be much lower than a king, in this particular game, the spade is the most powerful card.

God's Word is like the spade card. It trumps everything else because GOD is the Holy One. He knows no wrong and can do no wrong. His way is ALWAYS right (Psalms 119:160). And God's love and examples of love displayed throughout His Word is definitely the *trump* card over any other messages of love. When you have an accurate view of that, you, my friend, will live a life of extraordinary love! It won't matter if no one likes you in school, whether or not you have a boyfriend or high school crush. You will be feeling fulfilled by the Architect of Love!

 How does this relate to sexual purity?

Understanding what true love looks like paints a picture of what to look forward to when you choose to live in purity.

○ Sexual Purity has everything to do with experiencing only the best when it comes to love. You can't truly experience it without knowing God, the "Architect of Love." Since He designed love, one can't absolutely know what He had in mind without getting to know Him. When you get to really know God, you will be much more prepared and able to GIVE and RECEIVE love properly. You become an efficient vessel of the most perfect kind of love there is! This makes you a better daughter, sister, and eventually wife because you radiate the beauty of your creator. Everything about Him is pure, which means that since you've developed a relationship with Him, you also reflect purity. There's nothing more attractive than a girl who KNOWS who she is because she KNOWS her creator, and she's not willing to settle for anything less than what she KNOWS to be true.

Chapter 3

Receive The Gift of Love

> *This is how God showed his love among us: He sent his one and only Son into the world that we might live through him.*
>
> 1 John 4:9

When I was about the age of 7 or 8, Cabbage Patch Kid dolls were just coming out. I wanted one so badly I think I cried when I didn't get it for my birthday. My parents knew I wanted one. I even felt a little ignored by them because I couldn't understand why they didn't get it for me if they knew it was what I wanted. But I didn't know they were actually planning to get it for me all along – just not for my birthday, but for Christmas, a couple of short months away from my birthday. That Christmas I got that chubby, dimpled-faced doll with brown yarn for hair, and I was SO ecstatic. I adored that doll. I slept with it for several years until I thought I was officially too old to sleep with dolls around 11 years old or so. It's funny how we can get so attached to an inanimate object with no life in it. "Xavier," as I affectionately called him, was a gift of stuffing and material. No life was in it, and frankly my parents only got it for me because they knew I wanted it so badly. But they knew I didn't **need** that doll.

Have you ever gotten a gift you wanted so badly? What did you feel when you got it? Did you feel overjoyed? Did you feel a huge sense of gratitude from the giver of the gift? As I've gotten older I've learned the essence of a truly wonderful gift – the gift of Jesus. The gift of Jesus is my gift from the Father. He's also your gift. It's a gift much different from any other material gift you could receive!

Jesus is a gift that you not only want (whether you know you want it or not), but you also need. John said it perfectly when he saw the Savior Jesus coming toward him and said, "*Look, the Lamb of God who takes away the sin of the world*" **(John 1:29)**. Jesus coming to the earth meant that what God promised so long ago to all of creation was coming to pass. There would be a way that the sins of all men could be forgiven. When Jesus offered Himself as a living sacrifice for the forgiveness of your sins, the most amazing, valuable and precious gift was made available to you. Jesus, the gift of salvation, was given and you didn't even ask for it! But God knew you'd need it, so He gave it. Jesus knew and had the love of the Father flowing through His veins, so He unselfishly gave up His life.

"Greater love has no one than this, that he lay down his life for his friends" (John 15:13). Part of becoming a woman of purity is

> *When Jesus offered Himself as a living sacrifice for the forgiveness of your sins, the most amazing, valuable and precious gift was made available to you.*

receiving this unparalleled gift. Talk about the gift that keeps on giving! When you receive Jesus, and make Him the Lord of your life, you also are saying "Yes" to God's good and perfect will for your life! It's like a package deal! Kind of like those infomercials that come on T.V. "BUT WAIT, THERE'S MORE!" With this gift of salvation you will also receive unconditional and unfailing love, protection and guidance, strength and power, forgiveness and grace for all eternity!" WHAT A DEAL, RIGHT? The gift of

Jesus' salvation is the single most powerful gift that has ever been given!

When people receive this gift, it transforms them. They begin to think differently because they take on the mind of Christ. They begin to talk differently, because they speak with wisdom and authority. They love differently because they have the heart of God within. It's totally transformational, and this is why the gift has to be received before one can totally commit to a life of purity. Because once they do, they can see more clearly the holy path God has set for them. Did you know that God desires you to be holy as He is? (Ephesians 1:4) It's unrealistic to think that you'll ever be a perfect human being and never ever make another mistake in your life as long as we live in this very imperfect world. But God DOES call us to holiness. Holiness means we strive to be more and more like Him. We should answer the call to holiness for two reasons:

1. **Holiness is an extension of His love for you**. As your creator, He knows what you need most and what will bring you true fulfillment in this life. Living in sin brings destruction and death. But living according to His design brings joy and victory.

2. **Holiness brings glory to God**. When those who represent God's family represent Him... well, they make God look good! Don't you want to know that you're a great representation of the creator of the universe? Then you become a witness to the amazing gift of love!

So you see, it really is a package deal! You receive Jesus, and you also receive God's seal of approval. Does that mean that you become perfect all of a sudden? No, it just means that you become an open vessel for God to work His magic in your life. He won't force Himself upon anyone. But He certainly desires and longs that you will reach out and take hold of what He has for you. If you have already done that in your life, AWESOME! Continue to seek Him with boldness and tenacity. If you are not sure that you've made it a point to say, "Yes, God, I receive your gift of love in the form of Jesus' life that was given for me," then I encourage you to go ahead and do that in this moment. God's heart is for you to be in close relationship with Him. He's already made a way for you to have everything He knows you could ever want AND need. Would you let Him have your whole heart?

What does this have to do with sexual purity?

Knowing the Gift of Love is the first and most important love to have inside you will help you make the necessary decisions to stay sexually pure.

○ Jesus told the woman at the well who had several sexual partners that she wasn't really thirsty for natural water from the well (John 4). But the water He called "Living Water" would give her what her spirit and soul had been thirsty for. Jesus gives us what no one else can, and it can't be compared to a temporary, physical, sexual encounter with someone who IS NOT your husband.

Chapter 4

Overcome the Hurdles

> *Therefore, since we are surrounded by*
> *such a great cloud of witnesses, let us*
> *throw off everything that hinders and*
> *the sin that so easily entangles, and let*
> *us run with perseverance the race*
> *marked for us.*
> Hebrews 12:1

In America, the average amount of people who are physically active and exercise regularly is only approximately 25%. This has a direct effect on the number of sick and obese Americans. Do you exercise? Some like to ride their bike while others like to jog or swim. Regardless of the kind of physical activity, it's wonderful for your body to stay in shape, strong, and increase its ability to fight off disease. In fact, studies show that inactivity and obesity are directly linked to diabetes, heart disease, and even certain kinds of cancer. So you can see why it's important to stay physically active!

What about being spiritually active? Have you even heard of such a thing? Can you do spiritual exercises to stay strong spiritually? Can we do or avoid things to exercise our spirits and increase our spiritual health? OF COURSE!

The Apostle Paul was one of the most influential teachers of all things pertaining to Jesus and His message of the Kingdom of God. He understood how difficult it was to live for Christ in a time when His very life was in danger for doing so. So He on several occasions in the Bible spoke of "running the race," "perseverance in the race," and even "winning the race." Paul had to endure hardships because those who didn't believe in Jesus wanted to have Him killed.

His reason for needing to persevere is a little different from ours in our day. We need to persevere against the faulty, deceitful, and destructive messages from the very loud voices of the media

(T.V., movies, music, etc.) and those who don't believe in Christ. Hebrews 12:1-2 says, "*...let us throw off everything that hinders and the sin that so easily entangles, and let us run with perseverance the race marked out for us. Let us fix our eyes on Jesus, the author and perfecter of our faith, who for the joy set before him endured the cross, scorning its shame, and sat down at the right hand of the throne of God.*"

Paul's message tells us that to successfully run the race of life in Christ, we need to get rid of the stuff that makes us spiritually sick and weak. Instead of eating unhealthy food (sinful and false messages), we need to ingest healthy food (God's Word and the blessings of knowing His truth). Instead of being sick with the disease of sin, we live strong with God's help and power to endure the hardships life may bring.

It's funny to tell a story of when I ran track my freshman year of high school. It's funny now...but it wasn't funny at the time! I was looking forward to a normal day at track practice and getting ready to run my warm-up laps when Coach Miller called me to him. I noticed he was standing with the hurdlers and began to feel a little bit nervous the closer I got to him. When I got to him, Coach Miller said, "Hey, why don't you try these hurdles?" I immediately said, "No, I don't think I can do that!" Nor did I have any desire at all to jump over those hurdles! Something just really terrified me about hurdles.

Coach, however, was not convinced that I couldn't jump the hurdles, so he insisted I try jumping over three of them in a row over a distance of about 50 meters. It seemed I didn't have a choice, so I went for it. When I got to the first hurdle, I actually jumped clear over it! I'm thinking, "Well, that wasn't so hard!" Then I got to the second and cleared that one, too. Now I was starting to think that this wasn't as hard as I thought!

The third hurdle came, and I TOTALLY wiped out. And it wasn't pretty. My front leg had not cleared the hurdle, so I tripped on it, causing it to tip forward, and I basically went crashing to the ground on top of it. Can you say "OUCH"? I was pretty slow getting up and Coach came running to my rescue to untangle me from the hurdle. He asked me if I wanted to try again, and I said, "NO!" I never wanted to try jumping over any more hurdles for the rest of my life! But I have had hurdles of a different kind to overcome; hurdles that trip me up in my faith in God and from continuing to grow in Christ.

Numerous obstacles in this world can make it difficult to stay focused on the things of God. But just like in a normal race, even if you fall, you have to get back up and finish the race, regardless of the trials and hurdles. It's normal to trip up every now and then. But know that you have the ability to make choices that will lead you down roads riddled with obstacles or down roads pretty free of debris that could potentially cause you to stumble. Some hurdles are openly accepted and widely received as popular. Yet they directly go against God's Word. When they go against God's Word,

> *Numerous obstacles in this world can make it difficult to stay focused on the things of God.*

they also go against His best plan for you. Galatians 5:19-21 says, *"The acts of the sinful nature are obvious: sexual immorality, impurity, and debauchery; idolatry and witchcraft; hatred, discord, jealously, fits of rage, selfish ambition, dissensions, factions and envy; drunkenness, orgies, and the like. I warn you, as I did before, that those who live like this will not inherit the kingdom of God."*

There's a great list of hurdles right there! If you get tripped up on these things on a normal basis, purity really will be some unreachable thing in some far-off galaxy to you. So it's important to guard yourself. Guard yourself from taking wrong turns down paths that just lead to a dead-end trap. How you run your race determines the amount of love, fulfillment, joy, peace, grace and mercy you experience in life. Those are things God has already given you. But we sometimes relinquish it or give it up when we make decisions based upon sinful thoughts and messages. This is why you have to be extra mindful and aware of various hurdles so you can avoid as many traps as possible. The next few chapters will touch on some of the most influential hurdles which you may or may not already be struggling with. But know this: WITH GOD YOU <u>CAN</u> WIN THE RACE!

What does this have to do with sexual purity?

When you are aware of the obstacles or

hurdles that can potentially cause you to fall in your quest for purity, you can effectively prepare yourself to avoid them.

Chapter 5

Hurdle 1: The Media

> *Whatever is true, whatever is noble, whatever is right, whatever is pure, whatever is lovely, whatever is admirable – if excellent or praiseworthy, think about such things.*
>
> Philippians 4:8

Growing up, I was the kid who would go to school and hear all the kids talking about a certain T.V. show that was on the night before, which I hadn't seen because I wasn't allowed to watch it. My parents didn't allow me to watch shows that had things that could influence my brother and me in a negative way. "The Simpsons," for example, was one of those shows. Even though it was a cartoon, it was technically classified as an "Adult Animated" show. But because of the show's practice to make bad behavior seem popular and funny, my parents decided that would not be a show viewed in their household.

Your brain has the impeccable ability to remember things. It's an incredible muscle God put in us to hold tons of information. Well, the things we view in T.V. shows, movies, commercials, on the internet, hear in music, or read in books are all absorbed by our brain. And if it's in our brain, then our beliefs and behaviors can not only be influenced but also controlled by those things, even when we don't realize it! We can't control everything in the world, but we can control the choices we make regarding what we hear, read, and watch.

The media industry is a HUGE hurdle because most of the media channels do NOT carry any regard for what the Bible says or what God's standards are. Therefore, if you're constantly making choices to watch shows that encourage and glorify a teenage girl who smarts off to her parents all the time, guess what? You're probably going to begin to think it's okay for you to do the same. If you're regularly listening to music and watching music videos consisting of sexual content, guess what? You will probably be tempted to have sex before marriage, which of course leads to possibly getting pregnant or getting some STD (sexually transmitted disease). I'm being very real and honest with you because from the beginning of human existence, evil has always tried to tempt us with sin. The Bible says in Galatians 3:22, *"...the whole world is a prisoner of sin."* That means at every corner, we will be tempted by sin. This is exactly why it's so important to renew our minds with God's Word, full of truth and divine wisdom, to not be led astray by sin.

Hear me clearly. I'm not saying that every song that isn't about God or Jesus is full of sin. I'm also not saying every T.V. show is full of deceitful messages or every book is full of lust and perversion. What I'm saying is that you must be aware of the effect of certain shows, movies, books and songs that do contain harmful messages. A good standard to use as a measuring stick for your media choices is Galatians 5:19-21. The words used to describe those who won't inherit the Kingdom of God describe the kind of themes that may be repeatedly seen, glorified, or involved in certain kinds of media.

For example, there is a show that I'd heard of over and over last year. It was a fairly new show, and many of my friends on Facebook were beginning to watch and comment on it every week it was on. So I decided I'd check it out. Well, while it's highly entertaining due to intense story lines and plots, it's also full of sexual immorality, all kinds of impurity, envy, and selfish ambitions. By the time I watched a few episodes of it, I realized that something wasn't right inside my spirit. I noticed I began actually desiring for the adulterous couple to not be found out. WAIT! That's not what I should be thinking and hoping for. Glorifying a man and woman having an affair, regardless of how much in love the couple is painted to be is not excusable to God. NO AFFAIR IS OF GOD! This show has millions cheering and beckoning for all kinds of lying, cheating, and sexual immorality that make a large portion of the main story line of the show! I made a decision never to watch that show again. I admit that I got wrapped in it for a moment. But that is how sneaky sin is. It will have an effect on you without your realizing it until it's got you trapped in sin of your own.

Watching others celebrate sin, lust, impurity, and immorality will take its toll on you, so you must be very careful of what you set your ears to hear and your eyes to see. Don't be afraid to stick out when it's found out that you're not into that show or that book. God rewards those who diligently seek Him (Hebrews 11:6), and I can guarantee that choosing to use your time doing something that will glorify God instead of glorifying sin will be much more fulfilling for you in the long run.

> *Watching others celebrate sin, lust, impurity, and immorality will take its toll on you, so you must be very careful of what you set your ears to hear and your eyes to see.*

Anyone who knows me will tell you that I really enjoy music. Music is a very powerful force, and I know I'm not alone when I say it has the ability to really move me. However, most of the music on mainstream radio is about pursuing a romantic relationship with someone. Typically those songs are not singing about marriages and/or people who are seeking God for His will in their lives before they get romantically involved. Usually they're about "getting the girl" or "getting the boy" and they seem much more about lust rather than a holy, Godly love. So you want to be sure that you limit your music intake when it's not encouraging your relationship with Christ. Matthew 6:33, one of my favorite verses, tells us that when we decide to seek God and the things He has for us, we end up with all that we truly need. Actually, we end up with more than what we could think, imagine, or fathom! Why would you want to compromise the best God has to offer for things that were never meant for you to dwell on? I encourage you to find some favorite Christian music artists in your favorite style of music and explore the awesome feeling of connecting to Jesus through music.

Reading is a favorite past time for many people! I mean look at all the eReaders bought at

> *Why would you want to compromise the best God has to offer for things that were never meant for you to dwell on?*

Christmas time these days! In many cases reading really is power, as the posters say in libraries across America. But beware. All books aren't necessarily considered safe and are actually one of the toughest hurdles for many to get over.

Words paint pictures. Pictures arouse emotions. Emotions influence either for good or for bad. So reading is powerful. It's also true that what you read can become a stumbling block for you in your race to purity. What are you reading about? Are you reading about something being glorified that was mentioned in Galatians 5:19-21 like witchcraft or anything else that exalts itself above the one true God (idolatry)? Sometimes we overlook certain stories because of the incredible amount of entertainment we get from the story lines. But just because they're entertainment doesn't mean they are healthy to read. Regardless of the popularity, if it actively and consistently goes against what God instructs us about in His holy Word, you must ask yourself whether you should be reading it. I know of some amazing Christian thriller authors out there! They are able to write such intense and entertaining story lines while developing stories of faith. Those are available at any of your major bookstores, regardless of whether they are Christian or non-Christian. I love a good story, but I especially love when it encourages me in my walk with Christ!

Choosing to engage in different forms of media doesn't have to trip you up in your race towards purity. You just need to be aware of the messages within the choices you're making. Are they drawing you to or away from your gift of love? The awesome thing is you have the power to make whatever changes you need to! 2 Peter reminds us that God has already given us everything we need to live the kind of life He desires us to live. Use that power!

What does this have to do with sexual purity?

The mainstream media does NOT encourage sexual purity.

o   The mainstream media does a fantastic job of encouraging you to do the exact opposite of what the Bible encourages you to do. Sexual purity is a thing of the past as far as the media is concerned. The thing to remember is while all the romantic songs, T.V., and movie scenes are being played to woo you into buying more of their product and viewing more of their shows and movies, you're left to pick up the pieces of your heart. The entertainment is a money-driven industry, and your personal life isn't high on their priority list unless it means more cash for them. They play on your emotions to put money in their pocket. Don't allow their messages to influence you to enter into any kind of sexual relationship. When your time comes it'll be beautiful, but it should not be influenced by a popular storyline, scene, or song. God has a way of creating beautiful things of His own!

Chapter 6

Hurdle 2: Ungodly Relationships and Peer Pressure

> *Do not be misled. Bad company*
> *corrupts good character.*
> 1 Corinthians 15:33

Thinking back on my high school years, I can honestly say that outside my parents' influence the next biggest influence in my life, whether good or bad, came from my friends. You know what I mean, right? When you're a teenager, it's as if your whole world revolves around your friends. You want to be with them or talk to them all the time. And they could do no wrong.

But it was in Jr. High when I remember hearing my mom say, "Honey, maybe they just aren't very good friends." I was sobbing, one of many times, because one or several of my friends had hurt my feelings. When she said that, I thought, "What? NO! THEY'RE MY FRIENDS!" As if there could be no possible better choices out there than someone who would talk behind my back and play terrible jokes on me. Well, I was one who idolized her friends, and even when they hurt my feelings, I felt that was just the way friends treated each other.

It wasn't until a couple years later that I realized this wasn't true and that there were MUCH better choices available for choosing not just good friends, but GODLY friends. They helped me feel better about myself and also encouraged me in my relationship with God, even as a young teenage girl! Yes! There are people out there your age that can and will encourage you in your race towards purity.

A young man named Timothy, though he was young, risked his life to fulfill what he believed he was created to do. And he received great wisdom and counsel from others who were like mentors to him. One of the mentors instructed him to set an example for others in how he spoke, lived, loved, believed, and kept himself pure. Is it weird to you that **you**, even at a young age, can be a good example for others? Well, it's true! And one way to be like Timothy is by making smart choices of whom you spend your time with and whom you allow to influence you.

Timothy was a young but very committed teacher in the early days of Christianity, and Paul, his mentor, is known as one of the most valued writers of the New Testament in the Bible. The relationship between  Timothy and Paul is an amazing example of how influential we are as people. We are going to be influenced in some way or another, and be urged or pressured to do and or be certain things. When you feel the urge to do something positive, you've probably been influenced by someone else who is positive and does a lot of good things. But it is also that way with negative urges. Peer pressure usually describes negative things like smoking, drinking alcohol, dressing provocatively, and so on. However, there are good kinds of peer pressure as well! I'm all for peer pressure if it's the kind that urges you to be like Timothy and set Godly examples for everyone around you!

But what do you do with the bad peer pressure? What do you do when you have not-so-great examples around you in school or wherever? Here's the thing: young people really are some of the boldest people used in the Bible. David was a young tyke when he defeated Goliath. Esther was orphaned at a young age and later chosen by King Xerxes to be his new queen of Persia. Esther's influence on the king helped save the Jewish from being slaughtered. And let's not forget Mary! Mary wasn't much older than most of you reading this book right now, and she was chosen to give birth to the Son of God!

> *There is more to you than you know! Your young age doesn't mean that you can't be used by God and be strong enough to say no to the negative influences around you!*

There is more to you than you know! Your young age doesn't mean that you can't be used by God and be strong enough to say "**No!**" to the negative influences around you! Quite the opposite, rather. It's because you're young that you have the ability to be MOST influential. Don't let media fool you into thinking that all young people are good at is playing video games, idolizing rock stars, and getting into trouble. God has called you to be like Timothy! Paul even told Timothy to not let anyone belittle him because he was young. He told him that he could be an example in every area of his life, in fact. *"Set an example in speech, love, in faith, and in purity."* **(2 Timothy 4:12)** So be free to do some influencing of your own!

 But if you are in close relationship with someone like a close buddy or even maybe a boyfriend, it can be a little more difficult for you to keep from being the one being influenced for the worse. A super analogy is commonly used to clarify this point. Imagine yourself standing up on a chair. Your friend or whoever is an ungodly influence on you is standing down on the floor in front of you, facing you. You could certainly reach down and attempt to pull her up to your level, but not without some difficulty. However, it will be much easier for her to pull you down to her level, causing you to stumble in your race toward purity. This is why it's better for you not to be in close relationships with people who aren't striving for purity just as you are. They may not even want to pull you down

intentionally, but because they don't care about the same things that you do, it's inevitable they'll cause you trouble.

You may need to walk away from some relationships. This may happen more than once in your life as you're maturing in Christ and growing in your knowledge of God. It's not that you're "better" than them. It's simply a difference of priorities and standards, and if you want to be successful at accomplishing whatever God is calling you to, you can't afford to be pulled down. Again, ask God to strengthen you as you do it, but don't worry. God always sends those we need in our paths at just the right time. Like my mom encouraged me, there really are friends out there for you that have your best interests in mind!

 ## What does this have to do with sexual purity?

The old saying, "Birds of a feather flock together," is true!

o   If your friends don't see the value of purity in general, then they will not be much help to you in your race. If they are boy-crazy and always looking to get into relationships with boys (which are usually due to their own insecurities), it will be difficult not to fall into step with them.

Chapter 7

Hurdle 3: Sexual Temptation

Do not awaken love until it so desires.
Songs of Solomon 2:7 & 8:4

A 2010 study reported that 42% of teenagers ages 15-19 have had sex. That number is staggering! Further research shows this number is consistent with the increased number of teen pregnancies, abortions, and sexually transmitted diseases seen in teenagers in our country. I am not naïve. I do understand the temptation and the desires of sex...FULLY! But God warns us of this in His Word repeatedly and gives us instructions to be successful in not stumbling over this hurdle. The problem is if people aren't renewing their minds with God's wisdom and knowledge, then they're allowing their minds and souls to be affected by other things. One of those HUGE things is the media, of course!

Allow me to back up just briefly. Sex is such a special gift FROM GOD. Having said that, this gift was intended to be experienced between man and wife...ONLY. **(1 Corinthians 7:1-5)** Nowhere in the Bible do we read of God putting His stamp of approval on sexual relations outside the boundaries of marriage between a man and woman. I've searched for it many times and it's just not there, but I encourage you to not just take my word for it.

> *Nowhere in the Bible do we read of God putting His stamp of approval on sexual relations outside the boundaries of marriage between a man and woman.*

Search the Bible for yourself! It's important that you know, REALLY know, what God says about sex and immoral sexuality so that you have the keys to successfully leaping right over this hurdle without crashing and burning!

Back to the media and its influence regarding sex. The media gives us these messages about sex:

1. **"Everyone should be able to have sex with anything and anyone at any time." "Do what feels good!" "Go with the flow!"** These messages scream at us to go along with whatever temptations and desires our sinful or fleshly bodies lust after.

- No, God doesn't forbid us to have sex...unless of course you're not married to someone of the opposite sex. Just in case you are wondering, homosexuality is NOT a new or modern issue. God knew about it and has provided plenty of scripture which communicates His view on that as well. **(Romans 1:24-27)**

2. **"IT'S ALL GOOD!"** - There are no serious repercussions or consequences to consider when doing what the body craves.

- FALSE! I don't know anyone who enjoys constantly going to the local pharmacy to fill prescriptions to get rid of the rashes, aches, and diseases (some life threatening) from going outside God's design of sexual intimacy. I also don't hear many teenage moms saying they absolutely LOVE their life at 15, trying to raise a child by themselves because the boyfriend took off and isn't anywhere close to mature enough to be anyone's daddy.

3. "God made us as sexual beings. He wouldn't give us these desires unless He wanted us to experiment and enjoy it!"

- A hair dryer is a pretty useful and creative invention, but using it while sitting in a bathtub is NOT the way the inventor recommends we use it. Get the picture? God desires that we enjoy the gift and pleasure of a sexual relationship, but within the boundaries of a marriage between a man and a woman.

The Song of Solomon is a very different kind of book in the Bible. Many people don't quite know what to think of it, and most people don't quote verses from it. However, Songs of Solomon 2:7 and 3:5 gives some important words to heed. *"Do not arouse or awaken love until it so desires."* In other words, there is a time for you to "fall in love" with the person God desires for you to spend the rest of your life with. Be careful of awakening those emotions before it's time by entering into a premature relationship. Chasing after your crushes, reading romance novels, or watching movies that are pretty much based on romantic themes can all contribute to this. Those things will make it increasingly difficult for you to stay pure before God and keep those temptations from flaming inside your soul. While you may feel those things (having a boyfriend, reading romantic books, and watching romantic movies) are harmless, they are VERY influential (mostly in ungodly ways), especially to us girls because we tend to be led by our emotions. God placed emotions in us, and they're there for a reason. <u>BUT</u> God has a specific timing and season in your life for those emotions to be stirred up. So for now focus on this: protect your gift of love, guard your heart, and continue to strengthen your love affair with Christ.

> *So for now focus on this: protect your gift of love, guard your heart and continue to strengthen your love affair with Christ.*

It's so true that it feels good to be desired and pursued. That is a very natural feeling. The problem is that many times with teenagers when emotions are involved, they have the tendency to take over and self-control goes out the window! This is why you must be aware of all the hurdles to being tempted sexually. You may think being sexually tempted only happens when you are alone with a boy and you've begun to make-out a little, and suddenly one thing leads to another. Actually, being tempted sexually begins the moment you allow yourself to become emotionally attached to a boy. Even a little crush can turn into something you never meant to happen. It's not wrong to be attracted to someone. But if you allow yourself to repeatedly daydream about that boy, focusing your time and energy imagining yourself with him, it will become increasingly difficult to keep your heart and mind stayed on what God has to teach you during these years.

What can you do to stay focused on God and not give your thoughts over to the fascination of having a boyfriend? Romans 12:2 says to "renew your mind," which means to allow your mind to be transformed by meditating on God's Word. To help understand why that's so important, read the verse below.

"For the word of God is <u>alive and powerful</u>. It is sharper than the sharpest two-edged sword, cutting between soul and spirit, between joint and marrow. It exposes our innermost thoughts and desires."
Hebrews 4:12
(New Living Translation)

Even with the different sources of media, peers, and other voices encouraging you to act in a certain way and make unhealthy choices, God's rich truth being planted deep into your spirit is stronger than anything else! When you meditate and keep God's word at the forefront of your mind, it has the power to cut deep into the realms of our existence and actually take effect on your thinking and desires. It will keep you from sin because it will literally change you from the inside out. Move over, Harry Potter! Your magic can't touch God's Word! If you have not yet begun a regular Bible study habit, now's a fantastic time to do so! It will empower you, giving you the ability to do as Titus 2:12 says, which is to *"say 'No' to ungodliness and worldly passions and to live self-controlled, upright and Godly lives in this present age."*

 Time for a real heart-check. It's imperative that you really understand the following words. While God will give you the power and strength you need to overcome hurdles in your life, you will still need to be sure that you are positioning and setting yourself up to win the race. In other words, don't make choices to do things that you

know will cause you to be tempted to sin. It's kind of like this: I do not swim well and have not been very comfortable in deep water for a very, very long time. So how wise would it be for me to choose to go out as close as I can on my tiptoes toward the deep water? Even if I don't *intend* on taking one more step into the deep, most likely a wave will come along just strong enough to push me into the deep where I can't touch the bottom anymore. I'm left out there floundering, trying to get back to the safety of the shallow end where there was really no danger at all, thinking, "Why didn't I just stay where it was safe?" The reality is that *good intentions* are not foolproof. They don't always end well when you're teetering around shaky ground; you just may lose your footing and fall.

So this is why it's important that you re-evaluate. Where in your life are your intentions good, but you're getting very close to losing your footing? Many times, if a hurdler doesn't make it over a hurdle, it's because they miscalculated their steps somewhere **BEFORE** they got to the hurdle. What kinds of steps can you take to change a dreaded outcome of being entangled into sin? Something that I heard from a dear friend who'll tell you that she has made a lot of missteps in life is this:

"Sin will take you further than you ever wanted to go, keep you longer than you ever wanted to stay, and cost you more than you ever wanted to pay."

So it's time to get real with yourself and God and make some tough choices about where you are being tempted in this area of sexual temptation. Are you in a relationship that feeds your emotions but is weakening your God-given spirit? Romantic relationships at your age are virtually unnecessary and are best delayed until you're ready to seriously consider marrying someone. Until then, having a boyfriend really only seeks to fulfill your flesh longing to be wooed and pined over, which in reality usually only leaves you broken-hearted.

I know that for many of you this is very hard to hear, but think about it. If you didn't have a boyfriend, would sexual temptation even be an issue? Probably not, right? If you didn't have a boyfriend, would you be worrying yourself about how to keep him without falling into a sexual relationship with him? Probably not. Instead, you'd be wading around in the shallow end where it's nice and comfy, enjoying the water with your good friends and your feet firmly planted on the pool floor. And trust me, I am one who has tiptoed out there toward the deep with a guy intending on not getting swept away with the tide of ooey, gooey emotions, but that's exactly what happened. If I had just been real with myself and asked God to help me make better decisions along the way, things would've been different. However, that is the purpose of this book! To make you aware of these kinds of things so you don't have to learn the hard way. **So take some time now to have a heart-to-heart with God. What choices will you allow Him to lead and help you to make by His grace? Ask Him for the courage to do the hard and unpopular things and to strengthen you where you are weak. None of these things are impossible. Rather, Philippians 4:13 tells you that you can do anything with the help of Christ at your side. So let Him give you a boost toward righteousness and holiness and away from sin.**

 ## What does this have to do with sexual purity?

Allowing yourself to become tempted sexually is the first step toward engaging in sexual immorality.

o   The key is to guard your heart from relationships that throw you into a tailspin of emotion and fleshly passion. The best way to do that is to keep your eyes and heart on your Savior Jesus and become so overwhelmed by Him that no boy could tempt you away.

Chapter 8

Hurdle 4: Drugs and Alcohol

But I will not be mastered by anything.
1 Corinthians 6:12

The next hurdle is truly responsible for tripping up a number of folks, especially in the United States. Alcohol and drugs have the capacity to do major physical, mental, and spiritual damage. However, even with the obvious detrimental and fatal kinds of proof of the direct impact of alcohol and drugs, somehow most kids your age are still very casual and careless about their choices to "have fun" with it. If you want to get tripped up in running the race of living a life of purity in Christ, using drugs and alcohol is a sure way to crash and burn and crash hard!

Alcohol and drugs do not help anyone to make good judgments, nor do they aid in having much self-control at all. In fact it does the exact opposite. And while you may have some friends or even relatives who think that it's oh so funny to watch one another do and say stupid things while they're high and drunk, is there really anything funny about your friend(s) dying in a car wreck because someone couldn't make the decision to not drive while under the influence of some kind of substance? Not so funny then, is it? Not even a little bit! Yet teens still decide every weekend to go and get "sloshed" to have a good time or escape from the real world. This is exactly what your enemy, Satan, desires. The closer you get to self-destruction, the more power you give him over your life. Handing over power to him will surely result in your failing to accomplish the good and perfect will of God for your life. Game over.

One of the amazing things about God's Word is that it's applicable today. Even though it was written decades ago, it still holds value and is full of very useful info. It doesn't matter that there were no iPods, iPads, cars, or cell phones that have about 50 functions in 1 when it was written. The issues and trials we face today have been present since the fall of man. So we really have no excuse for not knowing what is acceptable in God's eyes and what isn't.

"The acts of the sinful nature are obvious: sexual immorality, impurity, and debauchery; idolatry and witchcraft; hatred, discord, jealously, fits of rage, selfish ambition, dissensions, factions and envy; drunkenness, orgies, and the like. I warn you, as I did before, that those who live like this will not inherit the kingdom of God. But the fruit of the Spirit is love, joy, peace, patience, kindness, goodness, faithfulness, gentleness and self-control. Against such things there is no law."
Galatians 5:19-23

The scripture above tells you very clearly that "drunkenness" (along with a host of other traits) isn't a quality that ends in experiencing the things He so deeply longs to share with you. And though the word "drugs" is not specifically mentioned in the Bible, it should be understood that drugs have many of the same affects as alcohol. They alter your ability to make wise choices and destroy the body. I had an uncle who never saw the age of 60 because of his close relationship with "the bottle." His liver was destroyed by years and years of alcohol abuse. Alcohol is very dangerous to the body when consumed in large amounts. Drugs very obviously have negative effects on both the body and mind. Is it any wonder that God doesn't promote using drugs, alcohol, or any other potentially addictive substance (cigarettes) that have been proven over and over to be destructive to you? It's for your own protection.

More specifically, let's talk about the image of a young girl like yourself who decides to drink excessively or do drugs. When girls get intoxicated, they are not necessarily very lady-like anymore. They lose all manner of charm and self-control, and become very sloppy and gross. Many times they end up doing things that leave them embarrassed and ashamed. Who is proud of that? Why would you choose to paint that image and reputation for yourself?

Sometimes girls drink to be popular with the "cool" guys. Those "cool" guys are actually more cruel than cool and care more about how many clothes you may take off while you're clumsily dancing with every guy in the place. They will probably want to take advantage of your inability to control yourself or make wise decisions and do whatever they want with you. So short of them pointing, laughing, and taking advantage of you, you can't expect much else from a crowd of guys at a drinking party. A question: are those the kind of guys you really want to associate with? Another question: where will that kind of behavior eventually lead? Rape, teen pregnancy, death...quite possibly. You are worth so much more. Will you treat yourself like the beautiful creation of God that you are? Will you be a good steward of the body God gave you, which is the temple of the Holy Spirit? If you don't respect yourself enough to, you cannot expect anyone else to.

> *No amount of alcohol or drugs will ever truly heal your wounds or make you feel better about yourself.*

Maybe you struggle with feeling like you are not worth much at all. Sometimes girls who don't feel really great about themselves drink or do drugs to suppress the emotions and pain of not feeling loved or accepted. So they receive attention when they're high or drunk, and that becomes their way of fighting against their hurts, fears, and low self-esteem. Know this: no amount of alcohol or drugs will ever truly heal your wounds or make you feel better about yourself. They will only add to your problems in the long run. There is a place in your heart that was only meant for the love of God to fill. When that place is left void, you will feel empty and hunger for acceptance. No substance, relationship, or material object will ever be able to please your soul in the way a relationship with God will.

Sometimes young girls begin to dabble in drugs and alcohol because they just don't understand the severity of how dangerous it can be. So they just experiment with it. I like to think of that scenario like this. Imagine that you owned a brand new cell phone with all the newest features and functions. One day, your little sister, who doesn't yet understand the monetary value of your new toy, decides to experiment with it without your knowing it. While you aren't looking, she takes it to the bathroom and decides to brush the buttons as if they were her little teeth with her toothbrush and toothpaste. Next, "TIME TO RINSE!" she says, and begins to place it under the running water from the faucet. By the time you realize it's missing, she's moved on to giving it a nice, hand-soaped bath in the sink. What a tragedy, right? Here's the thing...Little Sissy wasn't trying to hurt or break the phone. She was purely exploring and playing with the phone.

Many times we go about living life that way. We don't really intend on doing wrong or bringing harm to ourselves, but as we explore and "play around" instead of heeding wise instruction, we will eventually break down like I'm sure that cell phone did after a button brushing and warm, sudsy bath.

> *No substance, relationship, or material object will ever be able to please your soul in the way a relationship with God will.*

Please use this chapter as a huge "CAUTION" sign regarding drugs and alcohol. Exploring with them can lead to too many bad endings, and it's just not worth it. With close to $2 billion spent on alcohol advertisements every year in the U.S.[1] and new party drugs like Ketamine and Meth being introduced to youth, you have to be prepared and ready to handle yourself when it's offered to you. Radio, magazines, T.V. commercials, and peers around you may act like there are no dangers whatsoever. But the reality is that teenage drunk driving kills 8 teens **every day**[2], and it seems, teens are getting better at hiding drugs and their use of them from their parents, to their own detriment.

The danger is that these substances (including marijuana and cigarettes) physically and mentally alter and plays tricks on your body. Once the body thinks those substances are supposed to be present, it sends signals to your brain that you need more of it. Narcotics like meth, ecstasy, and LSD are becoming more and more addictive because the producers of these synthetic substances really only care about getting rich off your addiction. So the easier you get hooked, the richer they get. You can see why it would be helpful for you to be proactive about selecting whom you spend your time with, what you'll allow to be going on around you, and how you'll react to these hurdles if and when they show up on your track. This is one fall you definitely want to avoid!

 ## What does this have to do with sexual purity?

When a girl's heart is pure, she has no need for outside substances that alter her state of mind and physical well-being.

o When drugs and alcohol begin to enter one's life, it plays a pivotal role. A direct nose-dive is seen in the ability to make wise and healthy choices. Sexual purity is just one thing that is sure to be lost when drugs and alcohol are present...not to mention a lot of other things of eternal value.

Chapter 9

Hurdle 5: Pride

> *Pride comes before destruction and a haughty spirit before a fall.*
> Proverbs 16:18

Not very long ago I was running outside in our neighborhood, as I did quite frequently. I usually try to run about 3.5 miles, but I was trying to better the speed and timing at which I ran it. I remember thinking, "I need a good time to post on my Facebook page!" At the time, I didn't really think anything of that thought, but a couple of weeks later something dawned on me. My motivation for trying to run quicker was not for the sake of honoring God by taking care of the body He gave me and being more physically fit. It was so that I could receive compliments like "You go girl!" and "WOW! That's awesome!" from whoever might read my post on Facebook about my new record. I wanted them to be impressed with ME! I instantly became disgusted with myself and asked God for forgiveness and repented for being prideful and seeking glory for myself.

Did you know that boasting (or bragging), desiring glory for yourself instead of giving it to God, is a form of pride? Pride is a very sneaky and subtle weakness in us all as humans. Why? Pride can seem harmless and many times is hard to spot. However, it very quietly seeks to glorify and gratify selfish pleasures, desires, or ambitions. Pride always takes attention off God and onto someone or something else, many times...yourself.

You may also ask, "Why does God have to get ALL the attention?" God is omniscient, which means "all knowing." He knows all about you. He knows how you will behave when you turn your eyes away from Him and onto yourself. We seem to have a habit as human beings of forgetting what's really important. So we're reminded in Romans 12:3 when Paul says

"Do not __think of yourselves more highly__ than you ought" and also when James says in James 3:17, *"For where you have __envy and selfish ambition__, there you find disorder and __every evil practice__"* that we need to cease from trying to seek attention or glory for ourselves. After all, every good thing and ability we have is a gift from God. **(James 1:17)**

So instead of allowing yourself to get all puffed up from how pretty you look, how smart you are, how fast you ran, how well you sang, or how amazing your art is, you ought to remember to be thankful to God. Here is the danger: if we allow selfish ambition to take root in our hearts, before we know it there will be no room for honoring, worshipping, or seeking God. You will be too concerned about how others see you and envy you that it becomes difficult to keep your eyes on God. Even as a parent I have to remember to thank God for the wonderful qualities I see in my children. When people say, "You have a gorgeous-looking family!" I try to remember to say, "Praise God, we've truly been blessed." That takes the attention and glory off me and gives it right to God. That keeps me from caring too much what others say or think and more about what God thinks and giving honor where honor is due. Does this mean that it's not a good thing to ever feel good about something that you accomplished that's really good or impressive? No, just remember to thank the One who has graced you with the ability to do what you did. That will help you to stay humble and keep your inner thoughts in the right perspective.

Having a haughty spirit can be described this way. Let's say that your parents caught you doing something you know you're not supposed to be doing. That's the first part of being haughty: doing something without caring that it's wrong or even considering whether it's wrong. After you get caught, you sit there in front of them letting their words go in one ear and out the other. You don't really listen or allow yourself to be taught through this situation. Instead you roll your eyes, have a stinky attitude with your parents, and think very dishonoring thoughts about them in your head. You may even make up excuses in your mind as to why doing what you did was okay. This is a clear description of having a "haughty spirit." It started waaaaaay back in the Garden of Eden when the serpent told Eve that if she ate from the fruit from the tree (which she wasn't supposed to eat from), she'd be like God's equal. She ate it, mistakenly believing that it was going to make her more like God. She acted on a selfish ambition that actually did the opposite. Ever since then man has had a struggle with understanding the fact that God always knows better than we do. Just as in most cases, parents know better than their children and children have lots to learn from their parents. We as God's creation always need to understand the need to look to Him for wisdom, understanding, and guidance throughout our lives. However, many people think they don't need God or His Word that instructs us how to live. They ignore Him and His instruction, fueling the belief that they can be all powerful and all knowing like God. This is also called arrogance, which is the exact opposite of humility.

If and when you have the accurate perspective of who God is and give Him the respect and honor He deserves, it becomes very

> *We as God's creation should always understand the need to look to Him for wisdom, understanding, and guidance throughout our lives.*

easy for you to live life from a humble perspective. Psalms 24:1 says, **"The earth is the <u>LORD's</u>, and <u>everything</u> in it, the world, and <u>all</u> who live in it."** Having an accurate view of God means that you understand who is in charge, who you belong to, and who you will answer to when your life on the earth is over. And when you have that accurate view, it is quite hard to live life for yourself and for your own glory.

My personal prayer is that when I get a little too full of myself and become self-absorbed with what **I want**, that He will put me in my place and back to a place of total submission unto Him. Can you honestly say to God that you want His will for your life? Or do you want to just do what you want? If you don't feel you struggle with pride, take a deeper look at the times when you felt you deserved something that you didn't receive. For example, you didn't get the iPad for your birthday like you wanted. Did you feel even the slightest bit of anger? Ask yourself, "Who am I focusing on?" Is it yourself? Selfish pride is such a hard hurdle to recognize because it's very natural to focus on your own needs and desires. But Jesus says in Matthew 6:33, *"Seek first the kingdom of God,"* and He in his awesome, sovereign and all-powerful way will find ways for everything to work in your favor. Submit your ways to God; He's got your back! *"Humble yourselves before the Lord, and HE will lift you up." (James 4:10)*

Admitting that you are or have been wrong about something is VERY hard to do sometimes. It goes along with pride as well. But God is so pleased with us when we can be humble enough to admit our mistakes, ask Him to forgive us for those mistakes, and ask Him also for help in not repeating those mistakes. Know that He will help you, and He will show you. He gives us the ability to overcome our weaknesses. But if we're not humble enough to admit our shortcomings, He will not step in to show us the way. **(Proverbs 3:34)**

Let's take a little time to let down our guard and shed our pride. Pray the prayer below to let God know you really desire to run this race with Him and allow Him to lead the way.

"Father, thank you for your wisdom and knowledge and for showing me so much that I wasn't aware of before. You truly are a good God. I know that I've not been the most humble person. I've had selfish thoughts, ambitions and forgotten that you are the beginning and the end of all things. Please forgive me for being prideful. Holy Spirit, show me the issues in my life where I've been arrogant. I know that I need you more than anything else. Please be the center of my life. Be my all in all. Be glorified in every area of my life, Lord. I want your will to be done in my life and not my own. So just have your way with me, God. Amen."

What does this have to do with sexual purity?

Being humble, not prideful, is a sign of knowing that your life is not your own and that your body is not your own.

○ This causes you to have an honor and respect for both what's been given to you by God and for what He expects you to do with it. Humility means you can sacrifice what you "think" you want for now if it means obeying God. When you can get your eyes off your own emotions and feelings and onto God, He will honor your obedience and reward you in ways you can't comprehend.

Chapter 10

Keep Good Company

> *A friend loves at all times...*
> Proverbs 17:17

Friendships have proven to be one of the most influential relationships in a teen's life. You go to school with friends. You hang out with them on the weekends or during the summer days. You text THOUSANDS of messages to them in a month's time. Let's face it...your friends are pretty important to you. Is there anything wrong with that? No, not necessarily; as long as you understand the value and intent of a friend.

God has given us so many guidelines in His Word
about friends...the good ones AND bad ones. You
don't need to guess or wonder what God thinks
about this kind of relationship in your life. I told you
earlier how important my friends were to me and
still are today. My mom has had to console me many
times in my life because so many times I got my
feelings hurt, practical jokes and blatant neglect.
However, I have some awesome memories of my
friendships over the years as well. I have friendships
that have lasted for over 20 years! Then there are
those relationships that I was sure would last for 20
years but didn't. I must say that over the years I've
gotten better at picking friends and discerning good
friends from bad friends...THANK GOD! The book of
Proverbs contains scripture after scripture on
friendships. Chapter 12:26 says, *"A righteous man is
cautious in friendship, but the way of the wicked
leads them astray."* This tells us that we need to be
careful and make knowledgeable decisions
concerning friendships. The wrong kind of friend
could lead you down a wrong road away from purity
and becoming who God is calling you to be. Though it
may take a little while to find them at first, great
friends DO exist! The bad friends aren't completely
useless. They serve to show us why it's important to

know how to pick the good ones and maybe a hard lesson or two. But it may take weeding through a few bad ones to get to the good ones! Just take heart in the fact that God does desire for you to have friends. The following verse actually explains one reason why God desires us to find good friends.

> *"Two are better than one, because they have a good return for their work: If one falls down his friend can help him up. But pity the man who has no one to help him up!"*
> Ecclesiastes 4:9-10

A great friend can help you along the way throughout life. God created us to need one another, help one another, and build one another up, especially in the faith of Jesus Christ. There's actually a real desire within our souls to have others around us whom we can call friends, put there by God Himself.

Have you ever had a parent of a friend try to kill you because she was jealous of your closeness? I certainly hope not! Pretty dramatic, eh? Well, that is what David faced with his friend Jonathan. They were very close friends, and King Saul was so jealous of David that he actually plotted to have him killed. Even though Jonathan pleaded with his father to spare David's life, he wouldn't listen. So Jonathan warned David about the plot. What a friend!

I haven't had my life threatened, but I did have a situation with a father when I was 17 years old while living in a predominantly Caucasian (or white) neighborhood. I was part of a fantastic youth group where I had many Godly friends. We all hung out together and helped one another grow in the things of God. We had true fellowship with one another because we were like- minded and loyal to one another. A set of twin boys were part of this group of friends and had invited me to come out to their lake house to spend the day with several others from our group. Well, when the boys gave their father the list of friends who were coming, they were told that I couldn't come. Why? Well, let's just say that it had to do with the fact that my skin color wasn't the same as theirs. Their father didn't like the idea of his sons hanging out with an African-American girl. Not because I was a bad influence, but because he didn't want his sons one day developing a dating relationship with a black girl. When the boys told me this, I was crushed. I couldn't believe it! The twins felt horrible, but they assured me they were going to continue to be my friend. And they did just that because they valued our fellowship and they knew their father (who wasn't a Christian) was acting in ungodliness. Jonathan valued his fellowship with David enough that he stood for what was right and let no harm come to him. Now THAT is a great friend!

What about the not-so-great friends? We covered earlier how unhealthy relationships can be serious hurdles in the race towards purity. But let's talk briefly about what I like to call the "Cool Girl Syndrome." Many girls mistake "cool girls" for good friends. Their thirst to be accepted and feel important poisons their discernment to pick the right kind of friends. Instead, they pick the girls who get lots of attention from the boys, are the leaders of cliques, and may even resemble some teen Hollywood star.

Here's the thing...if you are chasing around girls like that to be friends with, you're in for a very rude awakening. Those girls getting attention from boys are most likely to be flirtatious, dress provocatively, and have very little self-value. They may be "pretty" on the outside, but because of a lack of identity in Christ, they don't have an accurate understanding that they're valuable without needing to attract guys to feel important. If they're in some popular clique, they're probably not the humble type. Usually people in exclusive "friend clubs" think a little too highly of themselves, so they limit who can and cannot hang with them. If they remind you of Miley Cyrus, Britney Spears, or Selena Gomez because of the way they dress, wear their hair, or do their make-up...RED FLAG! They have their eyes on something other than Christ, and where is that going to get them? Where is that going to get YOU by allowing yourself to be influenced by their ignorance?

> *The bottom line is HE ALONE is the only one you should be trying to impress anyways.*

You can be an example to those gals. Be the type that shines without having to show extra skin, be mean to other kids, or play the part to "look cool" by copying Hollywood's latest fashions. The reward will be much sweeter than any temporary acceptance. Your character is what matters to God. The bottom line is HE ALONE is the only one you should be trying to impress anyways.

The most important kind of friendship to pursue is the one between you and Christ. He is the one who paid such a high price for you. Not only did He choose to allow the Pharisees to spit in His face and the Roman soldiers to beat Him until His face couldn't be recognized, He went even further and gave His life for you. Jesus knew what He was going to have to go through. But He did it anyway. The greatest love of all was shown to you through the continuous unselfish acts of Jesus.

"Greater love has no man than this, that he lay down his life for his friends."
John 15:13

Can you imagine going through what Jesus went through for you for one of your friends? Not only is Jesus the one we should try to always be BFF's with, but He's also a great example of how to be a good friend to others. One who listens to what the Father God says. One who is humble, yet able to stand firmly for what's right. One who can think of others before herself. These are all great traits we see exemplified in Jesus Christ, which we can all strive to cultivate to be better friends. Take a few moments to talk to God about how you desire to be a better friend, and also ask for more wisdom and discernment in the area of choosing your friends. Maybe you need to renew your relationship with

Jesus and take your friendship to the next level. The great thing about Jesus is His arms are always open wide toward you! Remember, Jesus is the Gift of Love to you from your Father God. Nothing else compares!

 ## What does this have to do with sexual purity?

Allow Jesus to hold your hand throughout life and choose other like–minded people who have your back.

o   There is no friend who can love you more than Jesus does. He is the best friend you could have. Your parents, of course, care about you more than anyone else on Earth. But even they could never sacrifice to the degree that Jesus did for you. His life and death was all for little ol' YOU! If you let Him, He will guide you to that right guy you're supposed to share the intimate gift of sex with when you are married. Until then, listen to the advice of your parents and join hands with others who also want God's absolute best in their lives as well. They'll help you in the journey, and God has already hand-picked the best friends you could ever have to be your comrades along the way.

Chapter 11

Understanding the Heart of a Servant

*"Therefore, as God's chosen people, holy
and dearly loves, clothe yourselves with
compassion, kindness, humility,
gentleness, and patience."*
Colossians 3:12

My son is quite the crack-up. He has been living in
this world for all of 7 years, and sometimes he feels
he knows more than me. He is learning (sometimes
the hard way) that his parents do and say things that
will ultimately groom him to be a Godly man by the
time he's left our home and is on his own. He may
not enjoy the training and discipline, but it really is
because we love him too much to allow him to be

any less than who God is calling him to be. God is all knowing. He really does know everything! He knows what will happen on the earth from beginning to end, which is why He placed such great wisdom and instruction in His Word for us to heed. In Galatians 5:13-15, Paul states that if we don't love one another the way Christ instructed when He says, "Love your neighbor as yourself," we will eventually destroy ourselves. What God desires us to do is to be like the tentacles on an octopus and reach out from His heart, touching as many as we can to bring them to

Him. Ultimately God wants us with Him forever. It is impossible to do that if we are concentrated on ourselves. Our community and eventually the whole world will crumble if we all don't find ways to serve one another. It's plain to see throughout God's Word that servanthood is important to God. If it's important to God, then it has a connection to purity as well. Servanthood is volunteering your services, time, energy, resources, and gifts/talents for the sake of helping others. A true servant does something for someone else without expecting anything in return. If we dig into God's Word a bit, we'll find Philippians 2 tells us that Christ shows us the greatest example in servanthood by leaving His heavenly throne to take on the form of a man. He then allowed Himself to be bruised, beaten, and crucified so that WE might live. This is the ultimate example of service and humility. He made Himself a lowly man **(Philippians 2:7)** so that we might have a chance to be reconciled back to God. So since Jesus endured torture and death on a cross and gave us life, God gave Him the name above every name **(Philippians 2:9)**, which gives glory to God the Father.

> *This will lead to great reward in addition to transforming us into individuals who reflect the kind of purity Jesus had.*

Now...I'm not saying that you will have to do what Jesus did to be a good servant. I'm just saying that Christ paid the ultimate price to give God glory and obey His will. We need to be willing to do the same thing with whatever God asks us to do. When we serve one another in love, grace, kindness, humility, etc., we give God glory. This will lead to great reward in addition to transforming us into individuals who reflect the kind of purity Jesus had.

I find that when I'm centered on what God's will is in my life, I care less about whatever my selfish desires are. I become less involved in myself and more thoughtful of what's going on with those around me. This is why it's important to keep in our minds and hearts the examples of Jesus and many other men and women in the Bible. There we find that Jesus was driven by humility, compassion, and kindness like no other. It drove Him to do so much for the whole world. It drove Paul to continue working hard to build the early church even in the face of persecution and trials. Many came to know God as a result of Paul and Jesus' service to God and others.

Here is another thing to remember. We're not told to just have a little bit of kindness here and there, or every now and then do something good for some who needs it. Colossians 3:12 says, *"Therefore, as God's chosen people, holy and dearly loved, clothe yourselves with compassion, kindness, humility, gentleness, and patience."* Paul uses the word "clothe," which means "to put on." Think of it this way. You wear clothes nearly all the time, right? With the exception of the small amount of time you spend bathing, you're essentially clothed continuously. So you could say that clothes are pretty important to have because you're virtually always wearing them. Well, Paul purposely uses that verbiage with the believers at the church of Colosse to tell them that in order to be a holy and pure people of God, this has to be a huge part of who they are. It's not just something to remember at Christmas time or when someone asks for help. If you make this a priority in your life, you are serving others in kindness, compassion, humility, and etc. You're not doing it because you were asked or because it's a convenient time of year for it, but because it's a part of who you are and it is in your heart to do so.

 Remember, purity is really just a matter of the heart. When your heart is so full of God and His character, it becomes very difficult to do things outside His design. Besides that, your focus on God and others, instead of yourself, is a great deterrent from being too caught up in fleshly, lustful, and impure desires. Compassion and kindness are spiritual gifts, which means they are much more powerful than sin if they dwell deep inside you. We all can be tempted to sin and do things that go against God's standard. But the cool thing to remember is that when we live by the Holy Spirit of God, which includes gentleness, kindness, goodness, self-control, and love, we become less and less tempted to sin. It's actually like sin becomes disgusting and unattractive to us.

> *Those who practice humility and servanthood are much more fascinating than the most rich, popular, and gorgeous people who unfortunately seem to get more attention.*

One may think that if they don't steal from anyone, they're not hurting anyone. That's not necessarily true. Your neighborhood needs your help. Your school needs your attention. Your church needs what you have to offer. But if you never offer up what you have to give in service to God, you're taking away from what your neighborhood, school, and church can be. God has specifically given you unique abilities, ideas, and gifts to share with those around you. You never know who has been praying and waiting for you to come around with what you have. When you withhold what God has given you to share, you not only do a disservice to yourself and those around you, but you also do a disservice to God. I believe that those who practice humility and servanthood are much more fascinating than the most rich, popular, and gorgeous people who unfortunately seem to get more attention. Someone who is willing to put another person before themselves and sacrifice something for others looks like Christ. The world may not reward that kind of behavior, but God definitely does.

Nothing compares to the feeling you get when you know you've really made a difference to someone. It feels good because it's fulfilling God's will, which is for us to be His vessels of hope and love to one another. I'm sure many churches and organizations in your community are looking for volunteers to help serve food in soup kitchens, play with orphans in orphanages, or sit and talk or sing to the elderly in retirement communities. The list never ends. What would happen to your school if every student found some way of reaching out and serving others? Do you think that there'd be less time to do things that get your fellow students into trouble? If more kids your age were tempted to spend more time helping their neighbors than they do sitting in front of the T.V., computer, iPad, or Xbox, I have the sneaking suspicion there'd be less teen pregnancies, alcohol and drug abuse, and violence in schools across the nation.

Hannah: "MOM! Billy's not sharing!"
Billy: "Well, I had it first!"
Hannah: "So what? It's MINE!"

Billy: "So what? I'm the older one so I can play with it as long as I want!"

Does this sound familiar at all? Be honest. Let's admit that sometimes the hardest people to serve and share with are those closest to us. Why is it that we have the hardest time being polite and kind to those with whom we spend the most time? Perhaps we're so used to having them around that we relax on using our manners and being respectful to one another. Sometimes we even take our family members for granted. That means that we devalue their presence or the things they do for us because it's just a normal, everyday thing. For example, we don't think much of the fact that Mom or Dad is sure we have clean clothes to wear because they've always done your laundry for you. *No big deal.* No need to thank them for doing those kinds of things for you, right? Sometimes you may even get short-tempered with Mom or Dad just because they didn't pack the perfect lunch for you or they bought you the wrong colored shirt. That's a very normal thing that happens in homes. But how do you think God feels about how you treat the co-habitants of your home? In particular, what does the Bible say about how you treat your parents?

The best way to serve your parents is by obeying one of the 10 Commandments found in Exodus 20:12: **_"Honor your father and mother."_** You can serve them by honoring them. "Honoring our parents" has truly become a lost art among the youth in this country. Gone are the days where most kids refer to adults as "ma'am" or "sir," which showed honor and respect just because they were your elders (or older than you). To some that may not seem like a big deal. But the problems lie in the lost biblical concepts of giving honor to one another, especially those in authority over you. And when people lose

> _If you can't honor others, how do you honor God?_

the understanding of how important that is, you get what we see today: people talking badly about one another, calling names, fighting with parents and siblings, dishonoring those God has placed in positions of authority, from the President of the United States to the parent in your own home. It all is a very serious issue and directly affects your own relationship with God. If you can't honor others, how do you honor God? The word "honor" is mentioned almost 200 times in the Bible. You think it might be at least a little important to God that we understand the concept of honoring?

The verb "revere" is used many times to help describe the verb "honor." The definition for "revere" is this: **to regard with respect tinged with awe.** Allow me to give an example to help you see this more clearly. Think of someone you think is super **AWE**some and you think the world of him/her. Is it an athlete? Is it a popular singer, dancer, or actress? Maybe it's actually a member of your family! Whoever it is, imagine if that person came to your home to visit for a few days? How would you treat them while they were there? I bet you would be sure your house looked nice for them and if they needed anything at all from you, you would be more than happy to *serve* them to your best ability, all because you thought so highly of them and they mean something to you, right?

Now picture this. Someone walks up to this person you *love* and *honor* so much and spits in his/her face. That would be terrible, right? How dare they do such a thing! Don't they know who that is? Here's the thing: God feels this way about each and every one of us. He cares so much about us ALL! He desires us to show honor to one another because we're all His creation and not one of us is invaluable to Him.

Additionally, when you show honor to one another, it also shows honor to God. When you think of it this way, do you think it might help you to be nicer to your mom, dad, sister or brother? Spitting in the face of someone is a very blatant display of dishonor in any country. However, to God, something as simple as talking back to your parents or screaming at your brother or sister can be seen as equally dishonoring, not only to that person, but also to God.

How you treat those closest to you may be the ultimate test to how you will be able to treat everyone else, simply because it may not be easy. Let's face it, I think some of us show more honor to our pets than we do our parents who feed, clothe, and love us! Be kind to those closest to you. They are just as important to serve and honor as anyone else. Your sibling(s) may get on your last nerve, but how do you think they'll treat you if you treat them with kindness and honor? Begin to do some things for him or her and see how their attitudes change toward you. You may be surprised at how well you begin to get along as you begin to show love and honor for one another!

What does this have to do with sexual purity?

When you focus on treating others around you with kindness, compassion, love, and honor, you become less concerned with sinful things.

○ God desires for you to be used in the world. You will find fulfillment by reaching out and helping others, regardless of whether there is something in it for you or not. He designed you to experience an internal, spiritual joy from loving, serving, and honoring others. It just feels good. So good, in fact, that you begin to think and see people differently. You see life differently. You begin to understand that temporary, physical pleasures don't compare to eternal, internal pleasures. The latter are more related to the deep things of God that help make the world a better place. Immoral sexual relationships begin when a couple decides to turn a blind eye to the best that God has for them. But when you serve others, you serve God, which draws you closer to God. The closer you are to God, the farther away you are from sin and immorality as a whole.

Chapter 12

Preparing For A Wedding

> *"Marriage should be honored by all."*
> Hebrews 13:4

What girl doesn't dream about the day she walks down the aisle to one day marry the man of her dreams? To be finally joined with that perfect someone who will sweep her off her feet and live happily ever after, just like the fairy tales. Oh, I think I daydreamed for hours about one day meeting the guy that would hold my heart in his hand and would one day ask me to be his wife! When the time does come to plan a wedding, it seems the details are endless. And all of a sudden, your whole life is put on hold to tend to the perfecting of that one day! The building or church for the ceremony has to be selected. What music will be included? Caterers, florists, and the band for the reception must be decided. And of course, the dress...it has to be perfect so everyone will look upon you and drool over your beauty. Well, it is true that weddings are meant to be the celebrations of all celebrations. However, I'm sure that today, weddings are not viewed and/or approached in accuracy compared to God's original purposes and intent. Being a bride most definitely IS a big deal, but not for the reasons our modern culture has seemed to portray: for the glory of having all eyes on you and you having your moment to shine in your gorgeous wedding gown.

In a survey, reportedly 18,000 U.S. couples spent on average $27,000 on their weddings in 2011[3]. To help give you an idea of how much money that really is, it's just over half of the average annual income for Americans in 2011. So half of what the average American made on their jobs in one whole year was spent in one day on a wedding celebration. The survey also reported that was an increase from 2010 as a result of more money being spent on certain details, such as the cake, the band, and the decorations for a most fancy affair. Planning a wedding these days seems to be based upon gaining approval for grand appearances of the external kind.

However, the Bible shows us that the values of a marriage celebration are of a deeper and more spiritual kind. And preparing for a wedding begins long before that dream guy gets on one knee and proposes. Make no mistake. God DOES care about that day when you and the person that He has for you "tie the knot." But it's for reasons much deeper than your

> *And preparing for a wedding begins long before that dream guy gets on one knee and proposes.*

wedding being named as the most extravagant in the history of all weddings. It's because the whole idea of marriage was HIS idea. Next to our relationship with Him, a marriage relationship is the most ancient among the rest.

Way back in Genesis we see this in chapter 2, verse 24 when God says after He formed Eve from the rib of Adam, "**For this reason, a man will leave his father and mother and be united to his wife and they will become one flesh.**" God actually formed Eve so that she could be the wife of Adam. Not only in the beginning of God's Word do we see the intent and value of the joining of man and wife, but throughout the Bible it's also displayed over and over (though it is hard to find scripture expressing the importance of superficial details regarding the preparation of a wedding celebration). You have to wonder, what are we missing? Perhaps it's a lack of understanding of God's model of the marriage covenant and the seriousness of its intent. Perhaps, even from a very young age, we as future brides have had it all wrong from the beginning as to what we really should be looking forward to.

Before going any further, I want to be sure you have a clearer idea of what exactly is being celebrated in a wedding anyway! We celebrate, by description of the above verse in Genesis 2:24, the uniting of a man and his wife and their becoming one. In Malachi 2:14 marriage is described as a covenant. A covenant proves to be pretty intense in the eyes of God. It is a form of agreement between two parties. We're told in Hebrews 13:4 that the marriage covenant is to be "honored by all" and repeatedly through scripture, marriage is likened to a relationship to be had between Jesus and "the Church" (also called "The Bride of Christ"), which are those who believe in Him.

You see, marriages are SO important to God because He uses the marital bond between man and woman as a divine picture. It's a divine picture of Christ's relationship with HIS BRIDE, those He will one day come back for and fulfill His covenant – those who have prepared themselves for Him.

God desired man to have *"a suitable helper"* (Genesis 2:18) and *"a good thing"* (Proverbs 18:22), so He created woman. That alone should make you as young women feel valued by God! Within the marital relationship between one man and one woman lies also the divine design of the relationship between Jesus Christ and the Church, also called the Bride of Christ. The marital covenant is a solemn, binding agreement between man and wife to love and honor one another as Christ, the Bridegroom, loves and cherishes His Church, the Bride. His sacrifice on the cross is dripping with a deep love that Paul instructs husbands in Ephesians 5:25-28 to have for their wives. God's model for marriage is to be honored and upheld by a holy covenant never to be broken until death (1 Corinthians 7:10 and 39). Frankly, the Bible, from the beginning to the end, references these two marriages: the first marriage between Adam and Eve in Genesis 2 and the second between Christ, the Lamb, and His Bride, the one He is coming for in Revelation 19 and 22. The whole book is proof of God's model of His incomparable love and how to show that kind of love to one another. The celebration of marriage is such a big deal because it highlights the design of the amazing gift of love displayed in HIS–tory, God's story.

So we as believers in Christ are indeed the Bride of Christ! What a privilege that we are betrothed to the Savior of the world! Maybe you don't quite have the same view or value of yourself as God does. That's okay. It really is a process and no one is expecting you to just magically, "POOF", appear as the perfect pure and Godly woman. But I will tell you this: God honors every action you take toward being obedient to His Word. He will complete the work He began in you, as Philippians 1:6 says. And He really has given you everything you need for life and godliness, as 2 Peter 1:3 says.

Back to the preparation of a wedding! In a wedding, there is so much symbolism of purity on an outward scale. Unfortunately, much of this symbolism has just become tradition without meaning. In other words, the traditions are being carried out without any real care for the actual value of purity. Most people know that all the white in a wedding is symbolic of purity.

But how many brides who walk down the aisle in their pretty white gowns actually understand God's meaning of purity?

Purity is something God encourages us to go after because a pure heart is a blessed heart. When a man and woman who have been living their lives in purity unto God come together to marry, they are indeed blessed and their marriage becomes blessed. But it's not something that happens overnight. It's a process.

Did you know that in every process of purifying an element of some kind, it either has to be heated or

> *Purity is something God encourages us to go after because a pure heart is a blessed heart.*

broken down in some way? Silver is heated to high temperatures to burn away its impurities, which allows it to shine and reflect light. Before the impurities are burned away, the metal is dull and dark and could be mistaken for other metals that aren't valuable at all. Water goes through a very vigorous process of filtrating particles and chemicals that are dangerous if consumed. It has to go through a series of filters to break down the water molecules to its purest state so that it's safe for drinking. When something has been purified, the true value and intent for that thing can be experienced. It's no longer tainted with things that make it lesser in value. It's been made pure.

It's the same with you! When you take on your true identity of who God created you to be, you become pure and holy as He is holy. Don't get me wrong! As long as we live on this earth full of *im*purities, we will always be in a purification process. But living in Jesus Christ will indeed purify you as Daniel 12:10 states.

> *"Many will be purified, made spotless and refined, but the wicked will continue to be wicked. None of the wicked will understand, but those who are wise will understand."*
> Daniel 12:10

As far as white weddings are concerned, the origin of its symbolism is based on the purity and holiness of God and His powerful joining of a couple who vow to be pure in Him and to one another. And THAT really is a beautiful thing. Because they then get to experience the kind of love and relationship that began in His heart and mind, incomparable to what movies or fairy tales can try to make up or mimic.

Preparing for a real white wedding in God's eyes doesn't start at the proposal. It starts the moment you say "Hello!" to God's best for you and "So long!" to the things that keep you impure and living outside your true worth.

It's clear that a wedding is a huge deal! The preparation is enough to keep the mother-of-the-bride and her daughter busy for a complete year! What I hope you've learned from this week thus far is that the real preparation of a wedding in God's eyes has nothing to do with decorations, place settings, and bridesmaids' dresses. Rather, it has EVERYTHING to do with God and His beautiful creation of the union of two pure individuals for His glory. He cares more about the bride and groom's devotion to Christ, so that they are ready for what God has for them to experience together as one, than He cares for the wedding. He cares about their being ready for Christ to return when He comes for His bride, The Church. He cares more about them understanding the love of Christ so they can share it with one another and, in God's timing, their children. It's a preparation of the spiritual kind, not of the most expensive kind.

What does this have to do with sexual purity?

A real white wedding is about a couple who have dedicated their lives to purity unto God. This includes (but isn't limited to) keeping sexually pure until making a holy marital covenant.

- o The real preparation for a wedding should begin when you give your life to Christ and let Him know that you want to be a part of the Church, His bride. While growing in Christ, you become more like Him, which will also mean things like sexual immorality will be something you make wise decisions to avoid.

Chapter 13

Staying Sexually Pure in an Impure World

> *Flee from sexual immorality.*
> *1 Corinthians 6:18*

Sex. Sex is a big thing, but many times it's either not talked about or made to seem like a casual thing. Your parents may or may not have already spoken with you about sex. You may have even had a "sex education" course or two in school. Nonetheless, there's no doubt that sex is one of the most misunderstood subjects of all time. Sex is also called "the act of marriage."

Let's talk cocoa beans, shall we? Cocoa beans are one of God's numerous creations. In my opinion, one of the most yummy ones! Without cocoa beans we wouldn't have chocolaty desserts and drinks! I can't imagine a world without chocolate, can you? Cocoa beans can be used for health benefits as well! They are great for skin care and heart health, and they are super high in antioxidants. God really created something good when He made them. However, they can be dangerous to dogs, cats, and other animals. One can only assume that God made cocoa beans to be consumed and used by humans and not animals because their physical bodies cannot metabolize the caffeine as the human body can[4]. Cocoa beans are such a wonderful and significant creation to those for whom it was created. But outside that, it is quite hazardous.

Similarly, the act of sex, within its purpose and design by God, the Creator, is a beautiful and wonderful thing. When individuals have sex outside its original purpose and intent, they bring upon themselves problems they were never supposed to have to deal with. God made sex for a man and his wife to enjoy and experience together and only with one another. He intricately made the bodies of male and female to fit together perfectly so this can happen. He also grafted into the experience of sex a powerful spiritual bond that was meant to be shared only by a man and his wife joined in holy matrimony by God forever. God gave man and wife the miraculous ability to conceive a child through sex. It was supposed to be something very private and intimate for just a married couple to share in together. However, the world says something very different. And most of the world treats sex like it is not a holy gift from God at all. Therefore, we have

sexually transmitted diseases and abortions running rampant. Self-control isn't encouraged, and neither is anything else dealing with purity. However, we're told in 1 Corinthians 6:18 that committing sexual sin is a serious issue. ***"Every other sin a person commits outside the body, but the sexually immoral sins <u>against his own body</u>."*** Sexual sin affects a person mentally, emotionally, and physically for the worse. Individuals engaging in sexual activity outside the context of husband and wife are plain and simple abusing the amazing gift of God. They therefore bring God's judgment upon themselves as Hebrews 13:4 says: ***"Marriage should be honored by all, and the <u>marriage bed</u> kept <u>pure</u>, for <u>God will judge the adulterer and all the sexually</u>***

immoral." The thing to remember is that God gives us these warnings in His Word because He wants us to know how treacherous sexual sin is, and He would like for us to experience sex only as He designed it to be experienced.

When someone wants to hurt you, I mean REALLY hurt you, they will go for the deepest kind of hurt. They will do or say something concerning one of the most important or personal details of your life. Well, this is how your enemy, Satan, works. Satan wants to attack you in your most vulnerable places. He has attacked me in the area of my friendships by implanting so many lies in my head about me as a person and using some of my closest friendships to do it. He has mastered the art of taking something created to be good and twisting it to trick and deceive. Sex, I believe, is one of his favorite things to twist and degrade. Whatever he can do to get you to believe as many false things about it as possible, he will try it. That is why it's important for you to guard your heart. You have to protect it against his lies. When you successfully protect your heart, which essentially is your emotions and your mind or thought-life, you will win over the enemy's schemes every time. 1 Peter 5:8 warns us to be self-controlled and alert because "*your enemy the devil prowls around like a roaring lion looking for someone to devour."* That means that Satan is just waiting to catch you with your guard down so he can pounce on you and overtake you. The wise King Solomon encouraged, *"ABOVE ALL, guard your heart, for everything you do flows from it"* in Proverbs 4:23. He knew that decisions and beliefs are based upon what's in your heart, the place in

> *If the truth of God's Word remains at the center of who you are as a person, then you give your heart an ironclad protection.*

you that holds such intimate content. Satan knows that if he can get to your heart, he can get to you. Protecting your heart is essential if you desire to endure the quest for purity. So if Jesus has your heart, through and through, you will protect yourself against the enemy. If the truth of God's Word remains at the center of who you are as a person, then you give your heart an ironclad protection. Remember always that you need not fear the enemy when He (Jesus) that is in you is so much greater than he that is in the world! (1 John 4:4)

Abstinence vs. Sexual Purity

When I was a teenager, we were taught to abstain from sex or to practice abstinence to keep from winding up pregnant or contracting a sexually transmitted disease (STD). It was mainly for those reasons that we were highly encouraged to not have sex before marriage. Well, that is well and good, and teens could face those issues if they decide to engage in premarital sex. However, it doesn't really deal with the root of a much deeper issue.

You see, remaining "abstinent" is really just about making a conscious choice to neglect a physical desire

> *Sexual purity, however, is a product of having such a deep relationship with Christ that His power overwhelms impure fleshly desires.*

because of physical consequences. Well, here is the thing: fighting against a physical or fleshly desire with mere willpower and good intentions is a very difficult battle to win. Fleshly desires and emotions can be so strong that they can overpower whatever decision you made. Good intentions to remain a virgin until marriage is a nice idea, but many times is followed by failed attempts and promises. Sexual purity, however, is a product of having such a deep relationship with Christ that His power overwhelms impure fleshly desires. You have one desire: to please God with your life. Therefore your life also glorifies sex the way it's supposed to be glorified. Abstinence is more like you're just working really hard in your own power to not have sex in the midst of your really wanting to have sex. It has nothing to do with a deep longing to please God, which essentially leaves you powerless against the sins of this world. When Christ is at the center of your life, you don't have to fight against impurity because you have all you need to live a pure and Godly life (2 Peter 1:3). Because your heart is anchored to Jesus, your actions are not just good intentions. They reflect an internal spiritual power that looks like a giant against mere good intentions (Ephesians 1:18-19). People will look at you and wonder, "Why does she seem so happy without a boyfriend?" and "Why does she not seem to care about looking sexy?" Your answer will be because you know who you are and you know that nothing is worth degrading what God has for you. Your purity is sacred, and God designed you to live a pure life. Living outside His good and perfect design is equal to trying to climb a very high, steep, and rocky mountain. You will lose your footing, slip and fall, bruise and injure yourself along the way without the right tools. If you don't have what it takes to successfully get up that mountain, you'll eventually grow tired and weary of trying and give up, in spite of your "good intentions" to get up that mountain. "Good intentions" not seeded in Godly purity will most likely end in failure.

One sure way to stay pure in an impure world is to not follow after those who don't know and honor God. The scripture below describes these people well. Many are exemplified on television, in movies and in books. They just don't seem to care at all about holiness or purity. The following verse explains the minds of those who just don't have a clue about what God desires for their lives.

They are darkened in their understanding and separated from the life of God because of the ignorance that is in them due to the hardening of their hearts. Having lost all sensitivity, they have given themselves over to sensuality [earthly pleasures] so as to indulge in every kind of impurity with a lust for more.
Ephesians 4:18-19

So what are some practical ways that you can guard your heart and not give the enemy a foothold in your life in the area of sexual purity? Here are some things to remember and consider:

1. Generally, ideas enter your mind through your senses. When you see something, an image is imprinted in your brain. Hearing something has the power to either draw an image or idea in your mind. Touching something sends a message to your brain, and being touched in a certain way sends a certain message to your brain emotionally. So

> *What you watch, listen to, and touch has the ability to develop some kind of thought or emotion.*

you must know how important it is to judge what enters your mind through what you see, hear, touch, and how you allow yourself to be touched. What you watch, listen to, and touch has the ability to develop some kind of thought or emotion. What do you watch that persuades you to entertain thoughts of impurity? What do you listen to that ignites a thirst or lust to satisfy a fleshly desire? What do you touch or how do you allow yourself to be touched that can cause passionate feelings for a boy to arise in you? You must constantly ask yourself these questions to be sure that nothing begins to peck away at your heart.

a. Watching T.V. shows highlighting or glorifying romantic relationships between teenage boys and girls could eventually plant an early seed for romance in your heart. Next thing you know, you are longing emotionally for a romantic relationship of your own. Once that happens, your heart becomes divided. It's no longer solely set on Jesus because you're emotionally involved with a boy. This would be the first step toward impurity. Also beware of dedicating your wall space to pictures of "heartthrob" actors, singers, or athletes. When your eyes are allowed to gaze at and daydream about how gorgeous or attractive he is, you are also shifting your focus from idolizing Christ your Savior toward someone who doesn't even know your name.

b. Hearing certain kinds of music works in the same way. The popular theme of most mainstream music is based upon romantic relationships. This was a definite fact for me beginning in my young teenage years. There were those songs that led me to fantasize about having a boyfriend. Listening to them over and over again, little by little, worked at the ties that kept my heart pure. Music is powerful - period. I encourage you to listen to music that will encourage your relationship with Jesus.

c. Many times hand-holding seems so harmless and even portrayed as a "cute" display of affection in "innocent young love." God designed us to be attracted to the gender of the opposite sex. He did this for the sake of being able to share in marriage when it's time and to share in the act of sex. However, when a young person begins a physical relationship, even when it's just holding hands, it's like someone ice skating for the first time: they are going to slip on the ice and fall. It's not a matter of "if", but "when." It's not a matter of "if" hand-holding will turn into some much less innocent or cute behavior; it's a matter of "when." Keeping the "HANDS OFF" approach is always much safer in not arousing certain fleshly tendencies. You will have plenty of time to show affection with your future husband.

All of these recommendations are based upon the warning in Songs of Solomon 8:4. It warns young girls, "daughters of Jerusalem," about not stirring up love before it's time. It's best to guard your heart and keep those emotions and feelings untouched until it's time to commit to that one man God has for you to marry. It's not the way you see it happen in most movies, yet it's healthier and safer for you in the end. So if you haven't figured it out yet, within these recommendations is also the message of keeping yourself purely single until you are old enough to marry. It's not about just refraining from sex or staying abstinent. It's about dedicating your heart to Christ alone, something that's hard to do when a boyfriend is taking up space in your heart. Seek Christ the King first, and everything else will fall into place as God's will determines (Matthew 6:33). During these precious years, take steps in preparing yourself to be a truly beautiful blessing for the Kingdom of God first and, second, to your future husband.

> *It's about dedicating your heart to Christ alone, something that's hard to do when a boyfriend is taking up space in your heart.*

One more thing to add to ways to live purely in an impure world is to open the lines of communication between you and God. Getting into the daily habit of talking to God in some facet is another way to guard and strengthen your heart against sexual impurity. When the lines of communication are open and flowing between my husband and me, we are more often on the same page with one another. When it's you and God talking on a regular basis, you are more on the same page with Him. He always knows what's in your heart, but sharing it with Him draws you closer to Him, because later you see how your prayer life really begins to come alive!

Activating a prayer life deepens your level of intimacy with God and the Holy Spirit. You learn how to recognize His voice and receive direction about situations that may arise in your life. He's always ready and willing to draw close to you as you draw close to Him, as James 4:8 states. Sometimes I just casually call out to God and say, "Father," which is just like when a child calls for her mommy because she simply needs her. Just calling out for Him as my heavenly father is my way of saying "Father, I really need you right now." Some days it's just me saying, "Have your way in my life today, God." One of my favorite ways of communing with God is to sing to Him or even just listening to music about Him. We read in Psalms that when we tell God how thankful we are for Him and praise Him,

God's presence meets us wherever we are. It's really hard to explain, but it's like you suddenly begin to feel such love, peace, and joy that whatever problem or situation you were dealing with just doesn't seem to matter so much anymore! You feel like all is well no matter what you're going through! That's what you call supernatural. With God, nothing is impossible to conquer. Even sexual temptation!

 What does this have to do with sexual purity?

Understanding and respecting the original purpose and intent for sex will help you to desire the real thing and not settle or give in to sexual temptation outside God's design.

○ Part of many teenage girls' problem with sexual purity is that they listen to everyone else's view on sex, but don't consider sex from a Godly perspective. Therefore they also don't know the kind of lifestyle it takes to achieve sexual purity.

Chapter 14

Modesty: WHO CARES?

> *"Man looks at the outward appearance. But the Lord looks at the heart."*
> 1 Samuel 16:7

I was watching television one day and a commercial advertising a certain make and model of car came on. I don't remember much about the commercial at all, except for the fact that within the script of trying to sell a car, the word "sexy" was used. Yep! Apparently, we've gotten to a time in our world where a car can be described as sexy. On another occasion when the television was on, I overheard a commercial advertising for the "sexiest" cell phone on the market. Okay, so now on two separate occasions I'd heard of two objects with no personality, conscience, independent abilities or life be described as "sexy." Since then I've heard several other inanimate objects marketed in that way. Now personally, this kind of marketing doesn't appeal to me at all. However, I do believe that this is a sign of the times of living in what I call the "Sexy Era." Since the world we live in seems to be sex-crazy, companies actually believe that it will help them sell their products better.

You may or may not have heard the phrase "Sex sells." Unfortunately, it's true. Advertising and marketing agencies across the globe are always looking to grab consumers with modern, catchy slogans and stunningly visual images. And many of them are using seductive, lustful tactics to do it. In this kind of immoral climate the media could be in many ways responsible for sending wrong messages to you as a young lady about how to carry yourself. Instead of purity and humility, you learn of vanity and conceit. Please know this: a scantily dressed female holding a bottle of perfume with seductive eyes on a commercial is NOT who you should strive to look like or be like!

So what is modesty anyways? From most dictionaries, the word "modesty" is defined as decent behavior that doesn't attract negative attention to one's self. That "decent behavior" has to do with a lot of things: how one talks, how one manages their money, and how one lives in general. However, in most cases in our culture, when one thinks of "modesty" it has to do with the way someone dresses. Of course, it's important as well to be modest in life, period, and all the previous chapters are useful resources for modest living. Modesty of dress needs to be discussed in depth, however, because of the overwhelming amount of false messages that affect young girls through the world of fashion.

When you are out shopping with your friends or with Mom, what kinds of things are going through your mind in the dressing room? Are you wondering what your friends at school will say? Or maybe you're wondering what Bobby will think of your new outfit. Possibly you're not thinking either of those kinds of thoughts, and you just want to be comfortable and for your clothes to fit nicely. I'm sure you will eventually do what I do now sometimes when looking back at old pictures of myself, and think, "What in the world was I wearing and WHY?" I wore some things in high school that led me to wonder if I forgot to look in the mirror before I left the house or what? What I know now is that the most important thing to be cautious of when shopping is, "Can I wear this without dishonoring God?"

Carrying God's opinion into the dressing room with you is something a lot of girls may not do. They may carry their best friend's opinion, their mom's opinion, and maybe Teen Magazine's opinion, but not God's. Colossians 3:17 reminds us, "**Whatever you do, whether in word or deed, do it in the name of the Lord Jesus.**" In my opinion the verse means this: when you do what you do and say what you

> *You see, the enemy can use anything to sell you into believing a lie, even a shirt and a pair of jeans.*

say, it should carry Jesus' seal of approval. How do you know if Jesus would give the thumbs up on your clothing choices? We're definitely going to tackle that question, but I first want to emphasize that even when choosing what clothes you wear, be mindful of what God cares about. Some, not all, clothing produces unhealthy attention that makes you think or feel things that, instead of drawing closer to Christ, pull you closer to the things of this world, like vanity, selfishness, and unrighteousness. You see, the enemy can use anything to sell you into believing a lie, even a shirt and a pair of jeans. He's the king of deception and his ways are what's leading this "Sexy Era." My task throughout this chapter is to show you the ways he is at work in the world of fashion so you don't get caught up in believing you must sell yourself and your pure image to get what you want and be popular or successful. It's not true, and what

I also want women to dress modestly, with decency and propriety, not with braided hair or gold or pearls or expensive clothes, but with good deeds, appropriate for women who profess to worship God.
1 Timothy 2:9-10

God has placed inside you is so unique and valuable that it shouldn't be limited or defined by what you're wearing or not wearing.

Sometimes in life we can say one thing, but then do something that contradicts what we said. Unfortunately, we all have been guilty of this at some point. For example, in college during a brief period in my life, I would say I was a Christian if someone asked. But I remember several times when my behavior did not exemplify that I was a follower of Christ. It's because at that time, I placed other things in priority over my relationship with Jesus. He was not of greater importance to me than going out to party with my other "Christian" friends at that time in my life. That's an example of being superficial. I was trying to wear my Christianity on my sleeve by saying I was a Christian, but deep down Jesus was not at the center of my heart. If He was, I would have made more wise decisions and refrained from making so many awful mistakes. My

> *If Jesus is at the center of who you are, His likeness will spill out to the outside, too.*

"deeds" as mentioned in the above scripture did not exemplify one who professed to "worship God." At that time, I was worshipping myself by doing what I wanted and what was satisfying my fleshly desires. If Jesus is at the center of who you are, His likeness will spill out to the outside, too. If He's not, that will also spill out, but not in His likeness; it will show in the likeness of the vain and selfish world we live in. This is how your choice of clothes indeed does say something about yourself.

Before the days of T.V., Internet, romance novels, or radio, the majority of bad influences came from being around people who did not live righteously. No one could argue that this T.V. show was not healthy to watch or that song on the radio was raunchy and degrading to women. But Satan has been working his magic here on the earth for quite some time, so unrighteous activities were definitely able to be recorded in the Bible. The media is just a modern tool the enemy has been using to magnify his evil presence. However, the early church had its share of prostitution, drunkenness, and idolatry to ward off. And yet one of the things among the Jews regarded

as "unholy" had to do with what they ate! The Jews would actually classify someone as unclean or unholy if they ate a particular food, usually meat or a food sacrificed to idols. It had to do with some laws made back in the days of Moses.

However, Paul understood that after Jesus came and fulfilled the prophecy of the Messiah, whoever believes in Jesus could be made clean by His blood. It wasn't up to the food they ate or the sacrifices the priests made on their behalf for their sins anymore. But many Jews had a real problem with eating the kinds of foods that for years had been known as unclean. Because Paul didn't want to ruin his witness and ability to share Jesus with these new Jewish believers, he decided that it was more important to just honor them in their traditions. It was more important to him to keep an open line of communication about what really mattered – Jesus – than to argue with them over whether the food was unclean or not. So while he was around these newer believers, he would be sure that he didn't eat anything that would be offensive to them. Romans 14:20 says, "**Do not destroy the work of God for the sake of food. All food is clean, but it is wrong for a man to eat anything that <u>causes someone else to stumble</u>.**" I share this bit of info with you because Paul gives us a fantastic example of not letting your own actions cause anyone else to stumble while running their race.

Another reason why what you wear matters is because <u>it could cause others around you to stumble</u> in their

> *It's not just about what you're saying about yourself; it's also about what you're saying to others and, more specifically, what you're saying to guys.*

own walk with the Lord and their journey of sexual purity. It's not just about what you're saying about yourself; it's also about what you're saying to others and, more specifically, what you're saying to guys.

Paul talks about not being "stumbling blocks" on more than a couple of occasions in the Bible, so we must note its importance. You could do some things that could be a bad influence on those around you. We will talk about the specific effect on boys more in depth later, but know that immodesty and indecency of dress can be VERY destructive to boys and men. So if you care about your brothers in Christ at all and long for them to be successful in their journey of sexual purity, it's important you take this lesson of modesty to heart!

I'm old enough to have seen several fads come and go and experienced embarrassment when looking back at old pictures of what I wore in earlier years. Thank goodness the years of safety pinning and rolling the bottoms of my jeans are over. What a pain that was! The world has a lot to say about fashion *"faux pas,"* and with shows like ***"What Not To Wear,"*** there is no shortage of coaching on how to be fashionably sensible. With fashion do's and don'ts – like wearing socks with sandals to wearing the right pattern for your body shape – a person could earn a degree on how to be a fashionista! Though the advice might be helpful to know how to look good on the runway or the red carpet, it's not always helpful to know how to be modest in your clothing choices. There are quite a few modesty faux pas out there and, oddly enough, there aren't any popular TV shows to coach us on those. So it's up to mothers and Christ-like leaders to be sure to tackle the do's and don'ts of dressing modestly with young ladies today.

According to Wikipedia the term "faux pas" originated in France and actually means "misstep" or "false step"[5]. They used it when referring to loss of physical balance and also in a figurative sense, although it's used in our country most often when referring to a violation of what is deemed acceptable or normal. For example, an etiquette faux pas would be double-dipping your chip in the salsa at a party. It can be really offensive to others and has been deemed a social "misstep" when one double-dips. Two things strike me as interesting about this.

1. Many of us are much more concerned about misstepping in what the social culture says is a no-no than we are about what God deems inappropriate. We'll seriously consider what the world says about something in a heartbeat. Yet when someone recommends we take a more biblical perspective, we second-guess and hesitate to take it to heart.

2. Many "false step" when they just don't know any better. If one makes a choice to do something based upon a lack of knowledge, most likely they will not make a well-educated choice and will be guilty of a faux pas.

To those points I have this to say concerning dressing modestly. With both sensitivity toward the heart of God and the truth of who He says you are in Him, you should be able to steer clear of modesty faux pas. You know that nothing compares to God's approval – not catching the eyes of the boys at school or being named the "Best Dressed" in the yearbook. Those kinds of concerns and worldly cares dim our sensitivities toward God and lead to immodest choices of clothing and behavior.

> *This loud, and not to mention annoying, phrase, "If you got it, FLAUNT IT!" screams vanity and selfishness.*

I will be quite frank with you young ladies in this chapter. Because I am fired up about the lies the media is inflicting upon you, I am not going to sugar coat things to make sure you get the message.

This loud, and not to mention annoying, phrase, *"If you got it, FLAUNT IT!"* screams vanity and selfishness. For what other reason would you expose yourself other than for the sake of wanting to direct attention to yourself? Just because you are well-endowed in the breast category does not, I repeat, DOES NOT mean that you should show everyone by wearing low-cut tops. Yes, boys/men struggle to keep their eyes away from exposed cleavage. Some boys don't care and take every opportunity to lustfully look upon whatever amount of extra skin girls will give them to look at. But others really desire to keep their eyes from letting in impure thoughts and feelings. This is where not being a stumbling block comes in. Your future hubby will have the God-given right and pleasure of looking upon your bare body as much as he desires, but until then, I advise you to keep your bosom (including just a little show of cleavage) concealed.

The same thing goes for wearing short shorts, skirts, and dresses. I realize many of you are just picking out things that you think look cute. But allow me to inform you of the problems with clothing worn from the waist down. The higher the hems, the higher eyes will tend to wander. Where do your legs lead upward to on your body? That's right – your private area and behind, rump, tail, bottom, whatever you want to call it. When you wear shorts, skirts, and dresses that reveal lots of flesh, it's just a natural inclination for eyes to trail right on up that bare flesh to an area that's to be kept very private and personal. You would agree that if someone walked over to you and ran their hand up your bare leg to your behind that you'd feel violated, right? Well, why would you want someone's eyes doing the same thing? It's not only violating to you, but again, it is not helpful to boys in general and especially for boys who have a heart to stay sexually pure.

I am definitely guilty of some fashion faux pas, I must admit, in my 30-something years of living. I've worn white after Labor Day and allowed bra straps to be seen more times that I should have, mostly because I didn't realize it was a fashion "no-no." Now I think twice about the date when wearing white, and I have plenty of wide-strapped tank tops to cover my bra straps. But I was never pulled over by the fashion police or arrested for breaking these fashion laws. I might have been talked about behind my back about it, but there's no real penalty for those faux pas. In a way you could say the same about dressing scantily or immodestly. The fashion police won't come and give you a citation, but does that mean that it is harmless? Does that give you reason to carelessly throw on whatever you want? The following verse is one to learn and be mindful of, not only considering modest dress, but in general in your decision-making.

"I have the right to do anything," you say - but not everything is beneficial. "I have the right to do anything" – but not everything is constructive. No one should seek their own good, but the good of others.
1 Corinthians 10:23-24

Whatever you do, whether you could be thrown in jail for doing it or not, questions you should ask are, "Is this behavior constructive?" and "Is it helpful to others?" It doesn't hurt to be a little more thoughtful, but it could hurt to be careless!

I really want to repeat the importance of understanding that modesty is a matter of the heart. God is love. While the word love is tragically misused and misrepresented, **real** love – the kind that God is, gives, and created – cannot be duplicated by sexy dress and accentuated curves. Those things have nothing to do with God and everything to do with lust, vanity, and selfish gain. Some dress this way for no other reason than that it really does make them feel accepted and desired when they get attention.

However, this shows that these women don't believe there's enough inside them worthy of acceptance, so they resort to flaunting their outward appearance. It's heart-breaking, really, to see all the pictures on Facebook of females young and not so young, holding seductive poses pleading, "Look at me! See how pretty I am?" Sure, it may get some "Looking good!" comments, but it won't generate real love and fill the void of more of God in her life. Just because someone, girl or boy, likes how you've outwardly adorned yourself doesn't mean they will ever truly love you.

A passage of scripture tells us exactly what real love looks like: 1 Corinthians 13:4-8. It is a great checklist to use when you're trying to figure out if you are being truly loved and also to see if you truly love yourself! The two points I want to point out is that LOVE is not self-seeking and always protects. When you dress, hopefully you will choose to show love to yourself by not seeking to gratify the need for fleshly attention and protect yourself from negative attention. Show love to the boys out there who want to honor God and keep their eyes pure. Show love to God by honoring Him as you respect the body He gave you. Show love to your future husband by keeping your most intimate areas concealed for his eyes only.

 ## What does this have to do with sexual purity?

When a girl dresses immodestly, she attracts unhealthy attention and sends impure messages to boys who may want to approach her for lustful reasons.

○   Dressing modestly shows that you care less about who's looking at you and more about what you carry on the inside.

Chapter 15

Modesty: Modeling With Care

> *Don't let anyone look down on you*
> *because you are young, but set an*
> *example for the believers in speech, in*
> *life, in love, in faith and in purity.*
> *1 Timothy 4:11*

It's not news to the retail fashion industry that most women enjoy shopping. They know that, chances are, the next time you go to the mall you most likely will NOT come out empty handed. So they are sure to blast the T.V. with commercials and websites and magazines with ads to grab your attention. They would love nothing more than for you to spend your (or your parents') money on as much of their apparel as possible. They spend millions just to get you to walk into one of their stores. Then once you're in there, the use of outfitted mannequins and huge posters are used as another ploy for you to see yourself in their clothing.

Did you know that it is NOT the industry's job to dictate to you what you should wear? They believe that it is. But the reality is YOU have the power to judge what is wearable or not based upon your own trend and standards. You don't have to feel roped into buying anything just because the model on the poster looks sassy in it. They know that most girls want to look "hot" or "sexy" for the guys, so they market young girls in sexy, alluring poses to persuade you to purchase inside their store. But you are different! You are not going along with the pattern of this world (Romans 12:2). And guess what? If you don't like the messages a particular outfit or store displays, just don't buy it or shop there! If enough girls refrained from buying "Daisy Duke" shorts (REALLY short and revealing shorts), the

> *Did you know that it is NOT the industry's job to dictate to you what you should wear?*

fashion industry would have to stop making them and putting them on the market. It's that simple. You actually have the power to dictate to the industry what you care about in clothing. Isn't that kind of cool?

So let's talk about some specific immodest faux pas to be aware of!

Jeans

Everybody loves a nice pair of comfy jeans; well, those who actually can find a comfy pair that fit, I suppose. It seems like jeans are the most difficult kind of apparel to find that actually fits well! They are either too tight, too short, too long, or too low cut. It's tricky, but possible. I have gotten the same brand of jeans for the last 4 years because they are the only ones I've found that actually let my thighs breathe; they don't accentuate my high and curvy tooshie; and others can't see London, France or my underpants when I bend over. Here's another modesty faux pas concerning jeans...

Do you know what happens when you bedazzle and/or bling-out your bum? Well, it's obvious that those pretty little stones are meant to decorate. The problem is that your behind doesn't need decorating! As pretty or fancy of a design as your pants pockets may be with them, you're just asking for eyes to become attracted right to your bottom. Again, if you wouldn't want anyone to come and grab it, then you also don't want anyone staring at it.

And since we're on the subject of jeans, I have to interject something about a style of jeans that have been pretty popular the last couple of years...skinny jeans. I read in a 2009 article on fashion that young ladies ages 18-24 are heavier than they

> *Again, if you wouldn't want anyone to come and grab it, then you also don't want anyone staring at it.*

have ever been in past years[6]. With this said, wearing anything with the name "skinny" in it may not be the best choice of apparel if it means your thighs and bottom are hugged so tightly you can actually see the imprints of seams and creases on your leg when you take them off. Wearing skinny jeans should definitely be avoided if you are curvy anyway. Tight pants, period, just accentuate your curves and could draw negative attention or tempt your fellow brothers in Christ to inspect those curves. Skinny jeans might be okay if you can wear a long sweater or shirt concealing those curves from the thigh up.

But I'm pretty sure that defeats the main idea behind the creation of skinny jeans.

And here's another...

Posterior writing

I can't quite figure this one out. We were taught to read when we see letters. It's our natural inclination. What happens when letters are put on someone's rear end? PEOPLE READ THEM! Do you really want someone reading your posterior? This is never a good idea. The idea is not to drive attention to your private areas, ladies. Your bum is not a place for a reading lesson.

Workout clothes

You may have seen the scene played out on a T.V. commercial, show, or movie where the lady in the skintight spandex and halter top is jogging down the street and causes a man driving his vehicle to crash into the curb or fire hydrant. It's so typical of the misconception that all women enjoy having men gawking at them. I'm not saying it's not true that men gawk. What I'm saying is that it doesn't always have to happen that way. There are plenty of comfy, yet non-distracting, clothes to exercise in. What's heavily marketed is the kind of outfits that seem to get the most attention, like the tight, low-cut halter tops/sports bras and super-short shorts. However, we have plenty of alternatives to choose from!

One huge modesty faux pas that easily is overlooked because of the nature of this kind of apparel is...

Swimwear

I know, I know. This is really a hard one. But just hang with me for a moment longer. Up to this point, we've been talking about concealing your lady parts nicely and avoiding negative attention that may cause others to stumble. Just think about it. Why would swimsuits be an exception to this standard, especially when it has the potential to create the most issues of all? Swimsuits could quite possibly be the biggest modesty faux pas of all of the others previously mentioned and combined! No other type of apparel reveals as much as they do. If you didn't know, a large reason why teenage boys like to go to the pool is because of all the half-dressed girls running around with their bottoms hanging out, belly buttons unconcealed, and tops busting

> *Why would swimsuits be an exception to this standard, especially when it has the potential to create the most issues of all?*

loose in bikinis and high-cut suits. I have given up on wearing a normal lady's swimsuit. I'll share with you in the last part of the chapter some great alternatives. But I had an epiphany that I really am not comfortable in swimsuits. I am a married woman, and I really only desire one person, my hubby, to see me in all my naked glory. I don't even like undressing for the doctor! The standard doesn't change because you want to get wet and have fun in the sun. If you care about not causing anyone to stumble, then you should certainly care about not revealing so much skin, even in a swimsuit. If you really care about honoring your future husband by only allowing him to look upon you in a sexual way, then you will keep yourself covered until then...even at the pool, beach, or lake. This one is not easy, and I am fully aware of how popular it is to go shopping for that cute little swimsuit or bikini, but you really have to ask yourself: "What kind of attention am I drawing?" Is it Godly attention? Or is it lustful attention?

All of these modesty faux pas combined take some definite effort to battle against in this world we live in. The "sexy era" is in full force, but you can be an *exemplary* achiever by refusing to follow its habits.

Worldly standards will always take turns for the worst, but God's standards and ways are unchanging and constant. There are no fads with God. His only concern is that you know Him. And when you really know Him, everything else fails in comparison to what really matters. He is an **exemplary God!**

> **"Her beauty is her Godliness, and she ain't got to flaunt it 'cause it's obvious."**

I so appreciate Lecrae, a gospel hip-hop artist, for writing that line in one of his songs called "Identity." Besides being written in urban slang, it screams the message that I hope you are getting out of this book. The truth is that you are beautiful and become even more beautiful when you embrace all the amazing things God has put in you. You don't have to flaunt anything because you've placed your identity in Christ, not man. What you wear DOES reflect what's in your heart and whether you truly believe that you are who God says you are. Your real beauty can't be displayed by a short pair of shorts and a little (or a lot of) cleavage.

Let's recap some things to consider when it comes to dressing modestly.

❖ For whom am I dressing? 1 Corinthians 6:19-20 and 7:3 teaches that your body is not your own, but rather belongs to God and also to your husband-to-be.

❖ Does my clothing attract negative attention? Remember that when you look trashy or seductive, often you attract the WRONG kind of guys: the doggish, disrespecting kind of guys who don't practice self-control and let their lustful thoughts lead their actions. The other guys who care about Godly things will just "flee" from you as 2 Timothy 2:22 instructs them to.

❖ Who cares about "fashion"? They're always changing and the standards aren't based upon Godly kinds of cares. Romans 12:2 warns to not be conformed to the pattern of this world.

❖ Don't be selfish. Give guys a helping hand. Remember that guys are gratified by visual content. Don't contribute to any guy's struggles with lust and encourage them in their quest for sexual purity. (Romans 14:19)

Modeling with Care! – Part 1

~ Shirts ~

Factors to think about when choosing blouses, t-shirts, etc:

✓ **Tightness** – *Just say NO to a tightly packaged chest! A looser fit is best!*

    o   Pick a shirt that fits well and doesn't tightly outline your breasts.

    o   "Peeking Puckers" - Your button down shirt is too tight if it's puckering at the buttons. Pick a looser fitted button-down to prevent any opportunities for breast/bra/skin to be seen through the puckers.

✓ **Length –** *Rid the Mid!*

    o   Find shirts that have no problem covering belly button and tummy. You should also be able to raise your hands above your head, and your shirt will keep your belly covered. When you bend over or bend down to pick something up, your shirt should be long enough to keep your undies or "plumber's crack" from showing.

✓ **Cover the Cleavage –** *Put men at ease. Don't be a tease!*

- o Choose a shirt that doesn't reveal even a little bit of cleavage. V-necks and low cut shirts will usually call for layering with a tank top to prevent showing off your bust.

✓ **T-shirts and Text Across the Chest**

- o Be mindful of where the text is. Girls who have larger breasts should refrain from wearing T-shirts with lettering that adorns their protruding chest. It just makes breasts even more noticeable when the writing is being stretched out by a protruding surface.
- o Is the message on the shirt a modest one? Sometimes it's not the way you're wearing the shirt as much as the message. Words like *"Naughty"* or *"I'm a big deal"* are not representative of modest and humble messages.

Is it possible for someone who is modestly dressed to still be immodest? MOST DEFINITELY! Remember modesty is a heart matter. Things like your attitude and character can also be expressed outwardly by what's inside and should likewise be considered. It doesn't matter if you're covered from head to toe if you haven't learned the significance of kindness, servanthood, and honor. For example, when someone speaks to you, giving them eye contact not only is respectful to who's speaking to you, but it also shows that you are not insecure. Showing consideration and compassion for others is a very attractive quality on a young lady, as opposed to that girl who only cares about whether her hair is done perfectly and what time her favorite television show is coming on. In addition, a modest girl knows the difference between confidence and conceit. She knows that her talents and gifts are God-given and takes compliments with grace and humility, giving God the credit. These things make a young lady beautiful, but have nothing to do with outward adornment. Instead, her beauty is laced with the light and brilliance of her Lord.

Modeling with Care – Part 2

~ Bottoms ~

Factors to think about when choosing shorts, pants, skirts, and dresses:

✓ **Length –** *Less is more!*
  - o The less skin exposed the better. Choose pants that will appropriately cover thighs and, of course, your behind. If your pants are low cut in the waist, be sure you have a tank top or shirt long enough to be worn over waist so that when bending over you don't expose waistline, underwear, or "plumber's crack."

✓ **Tightness –** *Give me some room!*
  - o Choose nicely fit pants that will be comfortable as well as modest. Be sure that your rear end doesn't feel or look as if you had to squeeze it into whatever you're wearing, whether it be a skirt, pair of jeans (or any other kind of pants), dress, or pair of shorts.

✓ **Writing and Decorations –** *Keep words in books and fancy designs for your purse or bedroom wall.*
  - o Avoid wearing pants or shorts with writing or decorative designs on the rear parts of them.

This is best for keeping wandering eyes off that very private area.

My husband was not physically attracted to me when we first met in college. He saw me as a really "cool girl." I was pretty modest in how I dressed and I wasn't flirtatious at all to try to "bait" him, so to speak. Our friendship led me to see that he was definitely someone I would classify as "Godly husband material." After several months I was ready to begin dating him, BUT there was a problem. He still only saw me as a

> *He fell in love with me for what was inside, and THAT, my friends, would only get better with time because my heart belonged to Jesus first.*

sister-like friend. I had no desire to push him if he wasn't ready, so I just humbly kept my emotions to myself and patiently and prayerfully waited. To make a long story short, my husband eventually realized that I had all the Godly qualities he desired in a future wife. THEN he realized how attractive I was. I didn't lure him in by physically making myself alluring and sensual. I tease him about how long it took him and that it takes boys a little longer to "get a clue." But I'm so glad that it wasn't only about a physical connection for him. The physical details about me will change, and I would have to constantly compete with the latest fashions, as well as spend all kinds of money on anti-aging products and/or plastic surgery and Botox to stay "beautiful." He fell in love with me for what was inside, and THAT, my friends, would only get better with time because my heart belonged to Jesus first. My heart will continue to belong to Jesus first, and that makes me a better, more truly beautiful wife. I wish I always understood that was what truly mattered. I kind of learned this on a trial-and-error basis while getting involved with some pretty low-class kind of guys before I changed my standards for myself. But thank God for His grace, mercy, and wisdom that has allowed me to be joyfully married for 13 years now to an amazing Godly guy!

Modeling with Care – Part 3
~ Swim/Active Wear ~

Factors to think about when it comes to swimsuits and workout clothes:

Swimsuits

✓ **How much does it reveal?** – *Don't worry. Be happy!*
  - o Choose swim wear you don't have to worry about pulling and tugging on. Many times high-cut swimsuits ride up, and you always

have to pull it down to cover your rear cheeks. How about choosing a pair of surfer shorts that are the length of Bermuda shorts but made of material great for play in the water? Plus, they aren't nearly as revealing!

o   Pick out a fun swim tank that isn't low-cut to be sure that your chest isn't exposed and also sure to hold your lady parts in place so they don't fall out while having fun in the water. You can also wear a T-shirt over a swim top that isn't as modest.

o   Be sure that whatever kind of top you wear it safely conceals what happens to your breasts when you are cold. You may not know this, but this is another one of those things that stimulates guys, not to mention that it's embarrassing to you! So be sure your swim top's material is efficient for keeping your coldness a secret!

Active Wear
✓ **Tightness** – *Comfy yet cool!*
o   Choose exercise pants or shorts that don't cling and outline your curves, yet

the material is light enough to keep you cool while active. This can be rather challenging to find, but possible. You might have to choose a size larger than you would normally wear to keep them from hugging your curves.

o   While your sports bra should be worn to keep your breasts secure and stationary while active, pick a loose T-shirt that can go over your sports bra. Use caution with many of the exercise tops with bras built in. The tops are usually too tight and don't have the best bra support. Make sure your top allows you to move, bend, and stretch while keeping your breasts, underwear, and waistline fully covered.

✓ **Length –** *Give the gift of length!*
o   Shorts don't have to be high-cut or tight. Keep those thighs mostly covered with Bermuda shorts or, at the most, a pair of shorts with a mid-thigh cut. When you bend and stretch, your shorts will become shorter.

The Apostle John was a very good encourager to the early believers, and his writings are still very valuable to us today. Many kinds of things that the early believers dealt with thousands of years ago are the same things we are dealing with today! This is why the Bible is NOT just some ancient, useless book as some claim. Sin and lust was very much alive then, and it's very much alive now. Below is a scripture that John wrote to some very young men. Hopefully the boys who watch you do so because you're a leading example of purity and Godliness. Hopefully they're NOT watching you because you have chosen to expose parts of yourself that could potentially make them lust after you and disrespect your body.

"For everything in the world-the cravings of sinful man, the lust of his eyes and the boasting of what he has and does-comes not from the Father but from the world. The world and its desires will pass away, but the man who does the will of God lives forever."
1 John 2:16-17

It's important to use discretion according to a Godly level of standards. Be sure that you are humble enough to receive recommendations from older and wiser women of God. Many times their desire is to keep you from making some of the same mistakes they made. This includes your mother. It's her job to raise you up as a Godly young lady and also to protect you by giving you wisdom to live by. Using discretion and wisdom is sure to keep you on the right track when it comes to modest dress.

What does this have to do with sexual purity?

Many times girls dress immodestly because they simply don't know the difference.

o These guidelines and recommendations are to help you know how to make more modest choices in your clothing. As a result, you will be more equipped to avoid attracting lustful eyes, which many times can lead to early sexual temptation.

Chapter 16

A Woman of Purity: The Proverbs 31 Woman

> *Charm is deceptive, and beauty is fleeting; but a woman who fears the Lord is to be praised.*
> Proverbs 31:30

Do you ever wonder what God really had in mind when he created Eve for Adam? Oh, to be in the mind of God when He thought up this new creature! He gave purpose to everything He designed, and that certainly didn't stop at the birds of the air and the fish of the sea! He had an original intent and design for the woman as well. In Genesis 2:18 we see the purpose of a woman was to be man's helper. God created man, and then saw that he NEEDED a helper. In none of the other creatures He had created did He see an appropriate mate for Adam, so He created, from Adam, woman. She was a part of him, and in her creation man was finally complete. Not only was she visually and physically attractive to him, but she was also spiritually bonded to him. From the beginning God has given a mandate to women to be the perfect mate and helper for man. There within the creation of woman, man's purpose was also complete.

In Proverbs 31 we read of the kind of woman that fully exemplifies exactly WHY God created woman. She's a woman of so many qualities that the passage actually implies that she's very hard to find! It's true that women as described in Proverbs 31 are hard to find. Do you have any of the same traits she carries? Let's look at her character and see why the writer spent a whole chapter describing this impressive female! Look up Proverbs 31 and follow along as we pick out each valuable trait. FEAR NOT if you don't see these traits in you thus far. It's a process, and I can admit I'm STILL working on some of these traits myself!

Qualities of the Proverbs 31 Woman

❖ **She takes care of her family and faithfully tends to her household.**

(Prov. 31:11-12,15,21,23,28-29)

The scripture says that her family is able to speak well of her. They praise her. Why do you think that is? Because she takes such great care of them! Out of the abundance of love and purity in her heart she is able to give so much to everyone around her, but especially her husband and children. This makes her a fantastic wife and mom!

❖ **She is diligent and a hard worker.**

(Prov. 31:13-19,22,24,27)

Who says that a woman can't hold her own in the marketplace? This woman knows how to make deals and work with her hands to help bring income into the home!

❖ **She has the heart of a servant.**

(Prov. 31:20)

A giving heart is actually more attractive than a greedy heart. This woman helps out because her heart is to please God. God cares for the needy and poor, and so should we!

❖ She is clothed well inwardly and outwardly.

(Prov. 31:22, 25-26)

She wore purple gowns, which signify "royalty". She can dress in a way that even symbolizes she knows that she is a child of the King. Her character is laced with strength and dignity, though she speaks with kindness – not arrogance or boastfulness.

❖ She trusts God with all her heart.

(Prov. 31:30)

This is what makes her who she is. She trusts and honors God in every area of her life. This one trait gives life to all the others!

Chapter 17

The Purpose of Purity

> *"For I know the plans I have for you,"*
> *says the Lord. "They are plans for good*
> *and not for disaster, to give you a*
> *future and a hope."*
> Jeremiah 29:11
> (New Living Translation)

Earlier in this book, you learned that God designed the spiritual bond in marriage between man and woman to be an example of the kind of bond between Christ and the Church (or believers). And just as Christ has protected us from the price of sin (death) by dying on the cross and sacrificing himself for us, man is supposed to be that kind of protector at all costs in his expression of love and adoration for his wife. Likewise, the Church or Bride of Christ is supposed to be helping spread that message of love to all in the earth. Our lives are to complement and uphold the message of Christ, not compete with or divert attention from it. Jesus Christ said while He was still here in the earth that He would return for His people, His bride. But He also said that we should go into all the earth and share His message to everyone and prepare others for His return. What an amazing mandate the Bride of Christ has been given! Just as the Bride of Christ is to be committed and submitted to the Savior King, her groom who will return for her, we as women must also be committed and devoted to our husbands. In that commitment and devotion, man is able to function as God designed. He is able to be the appropriate kind of protector and spiritual leader for us when we effectively show our love and support. It's imperative, though, that we know how to do that according to God's design and not the world's design, which has been developed by the enemy.

The quest for sexual purity is all wrapped up in the divine purpose of a man and woman becoming one. It cannot be achieved without first understanding the importance of purity of spirit, soul, and body. Those realms of purity can really only be achieved by coming into a close, committed relationship with Jesus Christ. It's only through His salvation that you can receive the abundant life God always desired you to have. There you understand what real and true love is. There you receive peace and love that fulfills even the deepest parts of your soul. There you understand WHO you are because you understand WHOSE you are. Then

> *Sexual temptation is out there, but you were never meant to own it. Purity was always meant to be a part of your life.*

you desire the same things God desires for you. So you see, living a life of purity is encouraged by God in His Word because ultimately, you will live the best life you could live if you do so!

Purity may sound like it's next to impossible to attain. But the truth is it's already yours! Sexual temptation is out there, but you were never meant to own it. Purity was always meant to be a part of your life. It actually feels really amazing when you realize you're walking in God's ways because it just fits. But when you begin making excuses for something that you have even the slightest feeling isn't quite up to God's standards, something in you just doesn't feel right. Sexual purity may not be advertised on television or sung about in songs on mainstream radio. But I know many teenagers out there ARE living lives of sexual purity and effectively preparing themselves to be the best wives and husbands for their future spouses that they can possibly be! They're doing it by serving God and others. They're doing it by nurturing their relationship with their creator and Jesus, their Savior. They're doing it by spending time with other like-minded teenagers who want the same thing! Lastly, they're doing it by not allowing the rest of the world to dictate how to live their lives.

I'm going to leave you with one last impression about this *"Identity of Purity"* that I hope you claim as yours above any other. Proverbs 31:10

describes a woman of noble character who is more valuable than rubies. Did you know that rubies are actually more valuable than diamonds? Why is this, when it seems as though diamonds are the more popular stone? It's because of the rarity of rubies. Since true rubies are more difficult to find than diamonds, their value is more and sometimes even twice as much as diamonds. So it's quite fitting that the King writing this note of wisdom to his son would include that a woman of Godly character is not something that can be compared to just anyone. She's a rare find, but worth finding. If more young girls thought of themselves this way, we wouldn't see the epidemic of low self-esteem and self-respect we see today. The rate of cutting and self-injury would decrease. We would see more girls who package themselves as a treasure instead of trash. A girl of notable and noble character, who can find? She's definitely a ruby that stands out in the world. She's clothed in the light of Jesus, and her beauty goes deeper than skin deep.

 Could that be you? YES! IT'S SUPPOSED TO BE YOU! When you know how valuable you are to the

Creator of this universe, it becomes harder to disrespect yourself. When you know and believe with everything within you that the love of Jesus is more powerful than that of any boy, you realize that there's no good reason for dressing or acting in a way that degrades who you are. You really are one in a million! Don't let anyone convince you otherwise!

You really ARE worth more than rubies! God gave you a life to be lived to the fullest according to His glory. A newborn baby many times is described as a precious miracle. Just because that baby grows to become a young lady like yourself doesn't mean that her life isn't just as precious or miraculous. Remember that God's love doesn't change and His purpose for you doesn't change. He desires that you see yourself the way He does – valuable, precious, and beautiful.

Then <u>YOU</u> will reflect the true identity of...

Purity!

Endnotes

1. Campaign for Commercial Free Childhood: Intoxicating Brands: Advertising and Youth. June 2008 news article

2. http://www.learn-about-alcoholism.com/statistics-teenage-drunk-driving.html

3. http://gma.yahoo.com/u-couples-spent-average-27-000-weddings-2011-192005100--abc-news.html

4. http://www.ehow.com/facts_5900817_danger-excess-cocoa-powder-consumption.html

5. http://en.wikipedia.org/wiki/Faux_pas

6. http://www.filthylucre.com/fashion-industry-marketing-to-women

Dear Reader,

I hope that you have enjoyed reading this book! I would love for you to connect with me and let me know what you think! To connect and follow my upcoming projects, go to www.knowthespirit.com and find me under the "who we are" tab. You can also find me on the following social media.

Facebook:

Facebook.com/TheIdentityofPurity
Facebook.com/Rhianna.Sanford

Twitter: @PurityDefined

For booking or speaking engagements, please email me at:
rsknowthespirit@gmail.com

Keep your eyes peeled for "ELEVATE" my new worship CD to be released WINTER 2013! Thanks for reading and I hope to hear from you soon!

Sincerely,

Rhianna

Made in the USA
Charleston, SC
21 March 2014